# Metropolitan America: The Development of its Major Markets

By Juan de Torres

*A Research Report from The Conference Board*

# Contents

                                                 *Page*

FOREWORD .......................................................... v

INTRODUCTION—Michael E. Levy ............................... 1

1. MAJOR METROPOLITAN AREAS ........................... 4
   Statistical Measures for Defining Areas ...................... 5
   Classifying Metropolitan Areas ............................. 7
   Consumer Markets ......................................... 8
   Labor Markets ............................................ 10
   Industrial Markets ........................................ 12
   The Rise of Major Metropolitan Areas ...................... 14
   Nonmetropolitan America .................................. 15
   Conclusion: The City Mouse and the Country Mouse ......... 19

2. THE MANUFACTURING PHASE, 1880 TO 1950 ............. 20
   Prior to 1880 ............................................. 20
   The Starting Point, 1880 .................................. 23
   The Growth of Large Cities, 1880-1950 ..................... 23
   Urban Immigration ........................................ 24
   Intraurban Transportation ................................. 25
   The "City Beautiful" Movement ............................ 28
   Next Steps ............................................... 30

3. THE METROPOLITAN PHASE ............................... 31
   A New Beginning, 1950 .................................... 31
   Regional Characteristics in 1950 .......................... 33
   The Urban North in 1950 .................................. 33
   The Urban West in 1950 ................................... 35
   The Urban South in 1950 .................................. 37
   Overall Postwar Progress .................................. 38
   Urban Change in the North ................................ 40
   Urban Change in the West ................................. 42
   Urban Change in the South ................................ 43
   The Results in 1970 ....................................... 45
   Current Trends ........................................... 46

4. THE AMERICAN RIMLAND ................................. 50
   A Survey of the Rimland .................................. 54

Northeast Corridor ................................ 55
Springfield-Buffalo ............................... 60
Southeast ......................................... 61
Gulf .............................................. 64
Southern Pacific .................................. 65
Northern Pacific .................................. 67

5. THE AMERICAN HEARTLAND .................... 69
   A Survey of the Heartland ...................... 70
   Pittsburgh-Detroit ............................. 71
   Chicago-Milwaukee .............................. 73
   Border Region .................................. 75
   Northwest ...................................... 78
   Central West ................................... 79
   Southwest ...................................... 80

Appendix A: Definitions of Regions ................ 83

Appendix B: Statistical Methods ................... 89

Selected Conference Board Publications in Economic Policy Research 96

Bibliography ...................................... 99

Index ............................................. 100

# Tables

1. Relative Importance of Places of Residence, 1950 and 1970 .... 15
2. Distribution of Metropolitan and Nonmetropolitan
   Employment, 1970 ............................... 17
3. United States Urbanization, 1790-1950 ......... 21
4. Population and Employment in Northern, Western, and Southern
   Major Urbanized Areas, 1950 and 1970 ......... 33
5. Characteristics of 29 Northern Urbanized Areas, 1950 ........ 34
6. Characteristics of 18 Western Urbanized Areas, 1950 ........ 36
7. Characteristics of 13 Southern Urbanized Areas, 1950 ........ 37
8. Proportions of North, West and South Major Urbanized
   Areas, 1950 and 1970 ......................... 39
9. Characteristics of 29 Northern Urbanized Areas, 1970 ........ 41
10. Characteristics of 18 Western Urbanized Areas, 1970 ........ 43

11. Characteristics of 13 Southern Urbanized Areas, 1970 . . . . . . . . 44
12. Major Urbanized Areas, Frequency Distribution of Population
      Densities, 1950 and 1970 . . . . . . . . . . . . . . . . . . . . . . . . . . . . . 46
13. Annual Rates of Major Metropolitan Growth, 1970-1973 . . . . . . 47
14. American Economic Regions, 1970 . . . . . . . . . . . . . . . . . . . . . . 51
15. Northeast Corridor—Major Metropolitan Areas in 1970 . . . . . . 56
16. Springfield-Buffalo—Major Metropolitan Areas in 1970 . . . . . . 61
17. Southeast—Major Metropolitan Areas in 1970 . . . . . . . . . . . . . 62
18. Gulf—Major Metropolitan Areas in 1970 . . . . . . . . . . . . . . . . . 64
19. Southern Pacific—Major Metropolitan Areas in 1970 . . . . . . . . 66
20. Northern Pacific—Major Metropolitan Areas in 1970 . . . . . . . . 68
21. Pittsburgh-Detroit—Major Metropolitan Areas in 1970 . . . . . . 72
22. Chicago-Milwaukee—Major Metropolitan Areas in 1970 . . . . . . 74
23. Border Region—Major Metropolitan Areas in 1970 . . . . . . . . . . 76
24. Northwest—Major Metropolitan Areas in 1970 . . . . . . . . . . . . . 78
25. Central West—Major Metropolitan Areas in 1970 . . . . . . . . . . . 79
26. Southwest—Major Metropolitan Areas in 1970 . . . . . . . . . . . . . 81

# Maps

United States Manufacturing Belt, 1937 . . . . . . . . . . . . . . . . . . . . . . . 22
American Economic Regions, 1970 . . . . . . . . . . . . . . . . . . . . . . . . . . . 52

# Foreword

THE FIRST STAGE of America's industrialization and urbanization led to the growth of large urban centers in the "manufacturing belt" of the North. By contrast, the continuing urbanization of the last three decades has exhibited more diverse regional patterns. After World War II, manufacturing moved out of the North to the West and South, creating new urban developments in these regions and blurring the old distinctions among a manufacturing North, a rural South, and a West with great natural resources. By 1970, these traditional distinctions had become obsolete.

This study traces these fundamental changes in economic geography and in transportation and trade flows; it also sketches a new pattern of regional markets as revealed by the 1970 Census of Population and other current regional data. The results are, of course, tentative because America's economic geography lacks the high degree of centralization and the clear-cut hierarchy of urban centers that are common to most European countries.

In the past, regional markets have been less subject to thorough economic analysis than national markets (in part because of the poorer quality of the available data). Yet more and more important economic decisions will have to be made in the context of regional markets, as regional economics becomes more intertwined with our renewed interest in the "quality of life." The recent urban financial crises—particularly in New York City and New York State—have underscored the vital importance of the long-neglected truth that any efficient economic system has to be able to adapt to changing economic conditions and markets—this means *regional,* as well as national and international markets.

This report fills an important gap in illuminating the newly emerging patterns and interrelations of the regional markets in the United States. It builds on, and extends, previous work in regional and metropolitan economics that has been an important part of The Conference Board's Economic Policy Research over the past decade. Prepared by Juan de Torres, under the direction of Michael E. Levy, Director, Economic Policy Research, this study should prove valuable not only to scholars and state and local government officials, but to corporate planners and to marketing personnel of corporations that do not limit themselves to "national marketing" but have a vital stake in specific local markets.

DAVID G. MOORE
*Acting President*

# Introduction

A DECADE AGO, The Conference Board first recognized that economic problems and policies of state and local governments in general—and those of Metropolitan America in particular—would occupy a much more important place in the years to come. Hence, a new research program on Regional and Metropolitan Economics was developed within the framework of the Board's Economic Policy Research. This has resulted in numerous articles and monographs.[1]

This report presents the latest result of this continuing research effort. It draws on data matrixes and major findings developed in previous Conference Board studies in this field, but its most important contribution is an attempt to integrate the diversity and multiplicity of economic forces at the regional level through two basic theses: (1) Throughout its regions, the United States has become predominantly urban and economically more uniform, more stable, and more unified since World War II. (2) As a result of this postwar development, the traditional regional division into North, South and West has lost much of its economic significance and the substitution of a new division into a "rimland" and a "heartland" is likely to provide valuable and timely insights.

The first two chapters form the "prelude" to the main themes of this study. The opening chapter provides essential information on data, concepts and basic characteristics of the Major Metropolitan Areas.[2] The dominant role of Major Metropolitan Areas as basic consumer-market and labor-market areas is established and contrasted with Minor Metropolitan Areas and rural America. The second chapter outlines the first phase of U.S. urbanization from the 19th century until after World War II and the rise of the large manufacturing centers. This first stage of urbanization is identified with the expansion of U.S. manufacturing; hence the heavy concentration of population and economic activity in the Northern "manufacturing belt" prior to World War II and the high population density in the "old" urban centers.

---

[1] For a complete listing of these Conference Board publications. see the bibliography on pages 96 to 98.

[2] More detailed information and extensive statistical data on all U.S. Major Metropolitan Areas are contained in *Economic Dimensions of Major Metropolitan Areas,* Conference Board Report No. TP 18, 1968.

The last three chapters of the study contain its major and most original contributions. The third chapter describes the economic and demographic changes since World War II that have resulted in the predominance of Major Metropolitan Areas as population centers throughout the major regions of the United States—and the greater unification of the national economy. Net migration declined as a major source of urbanization and the U.S. population center has shifted closer to the country's geographic center. Service industries have gained in relative importance in the "manufacturing belt"—the oldest region of Metropolitan America—while manufacturing has spread to many of the newer metropolitan areas in other regions. In the process, urbanization has come to dominate nearly the entire United States and the economies of the Major Metropolitan Areas have become both more diversified and more stable.

As a result of these developments, the traditional division of the United States into the industrial and urban North, the poor and backward South, and the West rich in agricultural and natural resources, has lost much of its earlier significance. Thus, while the North remains the most "urban" region of the United States, it now contains many sections that are much less urbanized than the economy of California. The South remains poorer, in terms of per capita income, than the other major regions, but regional income differences throughout the United States have narrowed sharply. In fact, a few Southern urban areas have a higher per capita income now than some in the North.

While the third chapter documents the current dominance and the increasing economic unification of urban America, chapters 4 and 5 develop a new analytical division into a "rimland" and a "heartland," each divided into six subregions that are analyzed in some detail. (Incidentally, the concepts of "rimland" and "heartland"—while new and original in their application to the U.S. economy as proposed here—have had a long and fruitful life in European economic geography.)

The rimland is delineated here in terms of four Eastern subregions (the Northeast Corridor, the Springfield-Buffalo subregion, the Southeast, and the Gulf) and two Western ones (Southern Pacific and Northern Pacific). Common characteristics of both the Eastern and the Western portion of the rimland are a strong flow of trade along a North-South axis parallel to the coast; the predominance on each coast of one subregion with a huge conglomeration of population (80 percent) and the strong links of these dominant subregions with the rest of the world through overseas trade.

The heartland is also divided here into six subregions: The Pittsburgh-

Detroit area, the Chicago-Milwaukee area, the Border area, the North-west, the Central West, and the Southwest. The first three subregions, comprising the "old west," have a much longer history of industrialization and urbanization than the latter three which comprise the "new west." Consequently, the proportion of the population residing in Major Metropolitan Areas is much higher in the "old west." Among the chief characteristics of the heartland are the dominance of East-West trade flows, and an increase in urbanization that has not been fed heavily by foreign or long-distance migration (as has been the case for the rimland).

A few final words of caution are in order. In a country as complex and diverse as the United States, even the most guarded delineation of "universal" or unifying trends, and the most careful division of the country into economically meaningful regions and subregions, achieves clarification and new insights only at the cost of a certain degree of simplification. It necessitates painting with fairly broad brushstrokes that are bound to blur, or even at times to obliterate important details and distinctions. The Board's ongoing research in this area should lead to future reporting designed to fill in many of these details and distinctions.

Michael E. Levy, *Director*
*Economic Policy Research*

# 1.
# Major Metropolitan Areas

"If we could first know *where* we are and *whither* we are tending, we could then better judge *what* to do, and *how* to do it." (Abraham Lincoln, *A House Divided*, 1858)

THE DECENNIAL CENSUS OF POPULATION is a snapshot of a changing nation. The most crucial data are published with a one-to-two year lag, and the complete 1970 census was still not available in published form as of May 1975.[1] Despite the lag in time, the abundant materials contained in the Census provide an unparalleled opportunity for arriving at some approximation of *where* we are. This means an appreciation of the modern major metropolitan area, the most advanced form of economic development in the world at present, *whether* it be New York, Tokyo or Leningrad.

The term, "economic development," has become associated with the problems of "developing" nations, as if the "developed" nations had been frozen into an unchangeable pattern. In reality, this is not what is happening. America's metropolitan areas, for example, have been changing substantially over the postwar period. As late as 1950, American metropolitan areas were sharply divided between the large manufacturing cities, such as Pittsburgh, and the smaller trading cities, such as Mobile, Alabama. But, over the postwar period, the larger American metropolitan areas have tended strongly toward a more balanced economy. Large metropolitan areas are no longer as heavily specialized in manufacturing (or in one line of manufacturing) as they were in 1950, while many trading centers have drawn manufacturing investment. The result has been a growing similarity among large metropolitan areas, based on the increased diversity of their economies. This increased diversity that has accompanied growth implies a greater stability.[2]

[1] Great progress was made in the 1970 Census under George H. Brown, then Director of the Bureau of the Census, in speeding the availability of the information collected by enumerators through the use of properly programmed tapes. Thus, information on any *particular* community became quickly available. But the view of the whole depends on the use of maps and published data. These have been delayed because the 1970 Census contains much more data than the 1960 or earlier censuses.
[2] See Juan de Torres, "The New Reality of Major U. S. Metro-Areas," *The Conference Board Record*, June, 1975.

4

The present chapter deals primarily with *major* metropolitan areas in the United States, and secondarily with nonmetropolitan areas and *minor* metropolitan areas. Major metropolitan areas have become the most important part of the American economy. According to the 1970 Census of Population, they accounted for 54 percent of the population of roughly 202 million United States residents, while minor metropolitan areas accounted for 16 percent and nonmetropolitan areas for 30 percent.

## Statistical Measures for Defining Areas

One of the principal difficulties to be overcome in properly determining the size and shape of America's economic geography is that legal boundaries no longer follow economic boundaries at the local level. State boundaries have never coincided with economic areas but, in the past, the boundaries of towns and cities tended to approximate their urbanized areas, or their zones of influence.

Today, however, local government boundaries generally refer to some jurisdiction within a larger economic area. The main reason for this is that Americans have preferred to keep their local governments small. However, transportation has been revolutionized by the spreading use of the car and the truck and by great networks of roads for short-haul transportation. This in turn has affected the location of economic activity. Statistics for local governmental jurisdictions, while they may be of use to the employees and elected officials of these jurisdictions, have become less and less useful as measures for the economist, who is interested primarily in describing and analyzing *economic* areas.

The Bureau of the Census recognized this problem in 1940; at that time, it introduced the "metropolitan district," followed in 1950 by the Standard Metropolitan Statistical Area and the Urbanized Area.[3] An Urbanized Area is determined by a central city (or by twin cities) with a minimum population of 50,000, plus the population of all contiguous areas with a population density of over 1,000 inhabitants per square mile. The computation of population densities is an expensive process and, therefore, data for Urbanized Areas appear only once every 10 years in the Census of Population and Housing. Furthermore, it is very difficult at present to develop many types of data, such as income statistics, for

[3] "Metropolitan districts" proved to be an unsatisfactory concept because it was based on city and town lines, which were too numerous and often changed. Computation of data for "metropolitan districts" was an expensive and lengthy process.

Urbanized Areas. The principal advantage of the Standard Metropolitan Statistical Area (SMSA) is that its chief building block is the county, which covers a large area. SMSA's are composed of a county with a city (or twin cities) that contain more than 50,000 inhabitants, plus all surrounding counties that are economically linked to the central county. Data for the largest metropolis, New York, can be computed by adding ten counties to New York City. Most SMSA's are contained by two to four counties. Some, such as Phoenix, Arizona, consist of one county.

With far fewer building blocks, collection of data for SMSA's is much cheaper and more expeditious than for Urbanized Areas, facilitating the more frequent output of data, including annual data. Another advantage over the Urbanized Area is that the SMSA usually includes most of the population residing on the outskirts of Urbanized Areas, that is, people who have access to urban services but reside at population densities of less than 1,000 inhabitants per square mile. In the smaller SMSA's, the outskirts may account for a very large proportion of the population. Land prices are low and communication with the center is easy. Therefore, substantial parts of the population of these smaller areas reside at population densities of less than 1,000 inhabitants per square mile. Urbanized Areas tend to understate the size of modern metropolitan areas—by a small margin in the case of large metropolitan areas and by a large margin in the case of small metropolitan areas. The SMSA, however, includes the outskirts of Urbanized Areas.

Although the SMSA may overestimate the size of metropolitan areas by including some rural inhabitants, it is probable that this overestimate is so slight as to be insignificant in most cases. At first view, the term "urban farmer" may appear contradictory. Upon further consideration, however, it is apparent that the automobile and modern highways bring access to urban areas to many farmers within a radius of 100 to 200 miles of some metropolitan areas. This enables them to use and enjoy urban services and amenities.

The chief problem in using SMSA statistics is that no single unambiguous criterion has been found that properly identifies "accessibility." In 1950, the SMSA was regarded chiefly as a labor market. Thus, heavy commuting was used as evidence of linkage between adjoining counties. Yet, a business that settles in a metropolis can ship its products by truck to many areas from which it would be impractical to commute. Thus the exchange of goods and services within a metropolitan area extends beyond the journey to work—as do other journeys for medical help, recreation, etc.

The work of Brian J. L. Berry, among others, helped to switch federal statistical agencies to a less restrictive concept of "accessibility."[4] While an individual may not commute regularly to a city, the ability to use its facilities when he needs them means that he is not residing in a rural setting. Thus, many counties that would not have qualified under the criteria used for the 1950 Census are included under present SMSA definitions.

## Classifying Metropolitan Areas

There is a strong case to be made for making a distinction among metropolitan areas. First, the new term, "metropolitan," is stretched too far when it covers both the New York Standard Consolidated Area, with a population of 17,430,000 in 1970, and Bryant College Station in Texas, with a population of 57,173.[5] New York is 305 times larger than Bryant College Station which, in turn, is only 23 times larger than a town with a population of 2,500.

One avoids many difficulties by adopting a threefold classification instead of the official twofold classification into metropolitan and nonmetropolitan. The threefold division used in this study was developed in previous research at The Conference Board.[6] The first and largest sector consists of *major* metropolitan areas, that is, metropolitan areas with a population of over 500,000 in 1970.[7] This covers a range from the New York SCA to the Richmond SMSA in which the largest unit will be approximately 34 times the size of the smallest. The second sector consists of *minor* metropolitan areas in which the largest will be about 20 times the size of the smallest (containing a minimum population of 50,000). The remainder, that is, the nonmetropolitan sector, follows the official definition. (In a more detailed analysis, even this sector could be subdivided into a small-town versus a rural sector. The former would contain all the population living in Urban Places of 2,500 to 50,000 population,

[4] See Brian J. L. Berry, *Metropolitan Area Definitions*. Washington, D. C.: U. S. Bureau of the Census, 1968.
[5] Officially, Meriden, Connecticut, was the smallest SMSA in 1970. However, it is located in New Haven County. The Bureau of the Census still adheres to the practice of using towns and cities instead of counties in New England to define metropolitan areas in the decennial census.
[6] See Juan de Torres, *Economic Dimensions of Major Metropolitan Areas*. National Industrial Conference Board, TP 18, 1968.
[7] This report leaves out the question of why the dividing line between metropolitan areas has been set at 500,000 rather than, for example, at 1,000,000. See footnote 6 for source. See also Hans J. Blumenfeld, *The Modern Metropolis*. Cambridge, Mass.: The MIT Press, 1967.

7

while the latter would contain that part of the population of the United States that resides outside of SMSA's or Urban Places, now a very small minority of the total population.)

A strong additional reason for making a distinction above the 50,000 mark stems from market considerations, and it will become clear as we consider successively the three types of markets that are relevant to economic development: consumer markets, labor markets, and industrial markets.

## Consumer Markets

Consumption has a wider meaning in economic development than in consumer economics. It includes, for example, public safety. The security from danger to life and limb provided by firemen and policemen is a service to the individual, not only to the community. One gets a clearer view of what is meant by "consumer markets" if one contrasts them with "industrial markets." In his pioneering book on marketing, Harry F. Tosdale of the Harvard Business School told salesmen and sales directors that the industrial buyer is more rational than the consumer (see pp. 63-64 of *Introduction to Sales Management*). This fact cannot be denied. But if the causes are not elucidated, such statements may lend support to the myth of the irrational consumer whose wants are created.

The introduction of instant coffee illustrates the different positions of the industrial purchaser and the consumer. At first, the flavor of instant coffee was definitely inferior to that of coffee made from ground beans; but instant coffees offered convenience. Thus, the consumer had a choice to make, flavor vs. extra preparation time. Once a certain percentage had chosen the convenience offered by instant coffees and stuck to it after some experimenting, then coffee buyers could go ahead and buy low-grade, cheap coffee beans for making instant coffees. Finally, coffee planters were able to plant trees that yield low-grade coffees. Generally, the consumer has to balance more imponderables. But after a certain amount of "shopping around" and experimenting, the consumer has to make a choice and stick to it before the producer can plan his production. Sooner or later the test-marketing stage has to be abandoned so that the producer of a good or service can arrange production runs with some idea of the volume he is going to be able to sell. It is at this point that decisions about hiring workers and purchasing raw materials and machinery can be made. When the producer knows what the consumer wants, then he knows what *he* wants.

In the case of both consumer and industrial markets, establishments may either be located in a market or in relation to more than one market. In general, however, sellers will prefer to locate *in* a market if they sell to consumers. The reason is that, as a rule, selling to consumers involves the provisions of many services. Indeed, what is sold is often nothing but a service. There is a tendency in economics to ignore the creation of "place values" and "time values" because these are harder to visualize than an actual good, such as an automobile. Therefore, it is important to emphasize that no good or service is of value if it has been made available at the wrong place at the wrong time. If this occurs, then the seller may lower his price so that the consumer, hearing of a bargain, makes the effort needed to bring the product to *where* it is needed *when* it is needed.

Some errors are inevitable, *but* they can be corrected with lesser discounts in price in major metropolitan areas than in minor metropolitan areas. A small discount will draw many purchasers in a major metropolitan area where an extensive network of short-haul transportation connects a central business district and at least four shopping centers (e.g., Richmond, Virginia). Thus, an establishment that is located in a major metropolitan area has more options open to it, if it has miscalculated consumer demand, than one in a minor metropolitan area where there may be only one shopping center. It benefits from the Area of Dominant Influence (ADI, as measured by A. C. Nielsen Co.) of local TV stations and also from the metropolitan circulation of daily and weekly newspapers. If the establishment does not opt for lowering prices, there is often the possibility of quick cartage to another shopping center or to a number of small stores where the product or service may be in demand. This option is likely to be much more restricted by the narrower markets of minor metropolitan areas.

The demands of the consumer can be divided into habitual wants (such as milk for babies) and unusual wants (such as yoga classes for adults who feel too tense). With respect to habitual purchases, there is only a small difference between a minor metropolitan area and a major metropolitan area. However, the advantages of the larger market of a major metropolitan area become ever more important as the demand becomes more atypical. For example, a tobacco shop that specializes in custom blends for pipe smokers may be able to locate only in a major metropolitan area. Thus, a major metropolitan area offers not only better protection against unexpected fluctuations in habitual demands but it also offers opportunities for marketing many new or highly specialized goods and services that do not exist in smaller markets.

9

## Labor Markets

It is, however, in the case of labor markets that major metropolitan areas have the most decided advantages. Due to the high mobility of the population aged twenty to thirty, labor markets function with a high degree of economic rationality in the United States. The United States labor force—especially the younger and less experienced part—does not have the strong local ties that are found in many other nations. But, although interurban mobility is high in the United States, *intraurban* mobility is even higher, and the reason appears to be that America's workers encounter fewer obstacles in getting the jobs they want in major metropolitan areas where, as a rule, they can pick and choose from over 200,000 jobs.[8] In addition, while holding on to the jobs they have chosen, they are able to live in a neighborhood that suits their style of life.

The employer also derives many important advantages from having available a large pool of labor from which to hire. He can quickly find the techniques he needs, draw upon the experience of many more people, and avoid most of the sharp confrontations between management and labor that occur in labor markets where either management or labor find it easier to establish a monopoly. Today, an employer looks for a labor force with techniques, practical intelligence, and character. While wage levels are also a consideration, they have lost much of their importance because, over the years since 1929, intermetropolitan levels of personal income have been narrowed substantially.[9] (A migration like that of the textile industry from New England to the Southern Piedmont between 1920 and 1950 is not likely to be repeated today on the same scale.)

Techniques and practical intelligence can be subsumed under the broader notion of skills. "Technique" refers to skill taken in the narrower sense, such as the marksmanship of a hunter rather than his ability to track and kill animals. "Techniques" can be defined with relative ease and the Bureau of Labor Statistics (among other government agencies) makes available extensive data for the comparison of techniques. A major metropolitan area with a population of over 500,000—which means about 200,000 jobs—offers most employers a wide range and variety of techniques (unskilled, semiskilled and skilled). Many jobs require more than

---

[8] In the case of labor markets, size is not a continuously increasing advantage once a critical point has been passed. No one has yet defined this critical point, however. In some major metropolitan areas, such as New York, there may be more than one labor market.

[9] Unpublished data, courtesy of E. J. Coleman of the Division of Regional Economics, Bureau of Economic Analysis, U. S. Department of Commerce.

one technique, such as the combination of shorthand and typing. In a major labor market, it will be easier to find an employee with the right mix of techniques. Thus, at first sight, labor markets in major metropolitan areas offer an enormous advantage to an employer with respect to readily available techniques.

This is undoubtedly a real advantage but the absence of the right mix of techniques is no longer a serious barrier to the location of an establishment within a metropolitan area. It has its costs, but these costs have been reduced by two factors: the development of air transportation and the great advances that have been made in vocational training since World War II. Costly downtime, resulting from the lack of an on-the-spot "trouble-shooter," may be reduced by flying in an expert with the particular skill that is urgently needed.

Moreover, an *initial* lack of specific techniques need not seriously deter an employer from locating in a smaller labor market because this deficiency can be remedied in a relatively short time (a few months perhaps) by well-designed, intensive training programs. For the most part, the added costs are not prohibitive. In contrast, practical intelligence, that is, skill taken in its broader sense as an ability for some particular line of business, cannot be acquired quickly and at low costs. If it is not available in a metropolitan area, the employer may search for it in other parts of the nation and try to induce the skilled employees to move. The necessary inducements, however, may be more expensive than vocational education.[10]

The crux of practical intelligence is the power to apply general rules to particular situations. It is of particular importance in large or complex enterprises, where directives from the top must be phrased in general terms because of their application to varied and changing conditions. Successively lower ranks must be able to grasp these rules and apply them properly to more detailed and limited situations. If the work force does not have practical intelligence, top management will be forced to engage in tactical decisions and will not have time to consider strategic decisions.

Practical intelligence is promoted by a good educational system and educational attainment can serve as a rough guide to practical intelligence. But formal education is not sufficient in economic life, because the employer requires practical intelligence applied to some particular branch of industry. Thus, on-the-job experience in a particular organization is needed as well as formal schooling.

As an example of applied practical intelligence, consider the retail

[10] "Help Wanted," *The Wall Street Journal,* June 10, 1975.

clothing chain that adopts a policy of reducing the assortment of sizes it offers because short-term interest rates have risen, making it more costly to carry large inventories. Each store manager must decide which sizes can be dropped with the least damage to his sales. Salesmen, in turn, will have to change their selling style because they have less to offer. Thus, the general rule has to be adapted to the individual customer. If this does not happen, a strategic decision will fail even if it happens to be right.

It is with respect to skills in the broader and higher sense that a major metropolitan area has a decisive advantage. It may not be able to offer a labor force with more educational attainments than minor metropolitan areas. It can, however, offer a much wider range of experienced skills for an employer to draw upon. Such applied practical intelligence cannot be produced rapidly (even if one disregards costs). The worker, in turn, benefits from residing in a larger labor market. If he should become unemployed, more alternative jobs are open to him without having to change his residence or take a sharp cut in pay.

"Character" is even more elusive than "practical intelligence." In America's labor markets "character" takes on the meaning of fair play. Labor-management relations operate within the framework of the National Labor Relations Act (and its amendments), which permits adversary positions to be taken (within specified limits) by both parties in jurisdictional and wage disputes. In the absence of compulsory arbitration, great responsibilities are placed on both employers and employees to prevent adversary tactics from degenerating into vengeance, that is, the desire to teach the other party a lesson.

Although workers in larger labor markets may not be significantly more fair in this respect than their counterparts in smaller metropolitan areas, the situation is more stable because it allows for a diffusion of friction. A worker who does not "fit in," or who feels that his talents are not properly recognized, can transfer to some other establishment, often without loss in pay, standing or, even, seniority. In a small labor market, it is often difficult to make a new start.[11]

## Industrial Markets

Industrial markets are generally larger than consumer or labor markets. The latter are limited by the amount of time a consumer is willing to

[11] The history of American labor relations seems to bear this out. The most bitter conflicts appear to have occurred in mining, an industry that has to locate in small towns.

spend on shopping trips or an employee is willing to travel to work. At present, the commuter is rarely willing to spend more than one hour a day commuting to and from work. The 1970 Census of Population shows a decline from one-hour trips in 1950 to one-half hours in 1970. Two-hour trips to work were a decided minority in 1950, but they still existed. At present, they have virtually disappeared.

The shopping trip is more variable. A shopper might be willing to spend a whole day for a "big-ticket" item. But for the many items with small price tags that are habitually purchased, the consumer will rarely be willing to spend the greater part of the day traveling among stores, unless there is a very substantial price advantage.

However, the effective radius over which it is worth shipping industrial goods probably extends at least as far as the distance that can be covered by a truck in one round trip during an entire working day (taking into account the time spent on loading and unloading, paperwork, routing, etc.). Thus, as a rule major metropolitan areas are likely to be contained by industrial markets despite their large size, whereas in the case of consumer and labor markets they are likely to contain more than one. For example, the Cleveland-Akron SCA contains at least four consumer markets (Lorain, Cleveland west and east of the Cuyahoga River, and Akron) and two labor markets (Cleveland and Akron) but, although this major metropolitan area was the ninth largest in the United States in terms of employment in 1972 (1.1 million workers), it was contained by a larger industrial market that included Toledo and Youngstown-Warren (two other major metropolitan areas in Ohio), Mansfield and Canton, Ohio and Erie, Pennsylvania (three minor metropolitan areas), plus Sandusky, a large Ohio town. The larger size of industrial markets means that a large number of minor metropolitan areas cannot be distinguished in this respect from major metropolitan areas. These are the satellites that one often finds around major metropolitan areas. Such satellites will have narrow consumer and labor markets but the industrial markets on which they can rely will be as large as those of major metropolitan areas (with the possible exception of the three biggest, New York, Los Angeles, and Chicago).

With respect to industrial markets, moreover, minor metropolitan areas are not wholly at a disadvantage compared with major metropolitan areas. They will be at a disadvantage with respect to tools, but they will often have an advantage with respect to raw materials. Where tools are concerned, a major metropolitan area is likely to enjoy an advantage over minor metropolitan areas. Modern business uses complex, sophisticated

13

equipment, whether it is a bank using computers, or a steel mill using an oxygen furnace. Downtime on any such equipment can be very costly and can be avoided in a minor metropolitan area only by keeping a large stock of replacement parts. A major metropolitan area provides a larger market for such equipment, facilitating alternative sources of supply and a ready availability of parts. Air freight reduces some of these advantages, but it does not eliminate them. Only by being a satellite of a larger metropolitan area can a minor metropolitan area avoid this disadvantage entirely.

With respect to raw materials, however, minor metropolitan areas will often have an advantage over major metropolitan areas because many industrial processes reduce the weight of the raw material that is being processed. Thus, the production of copper requires separation, smelting and refining. Each one of these operations reduces the weight and bulk of what comes up from the mine. Furthermore, energy often comes in the form of a raw material that is used in fabrication but does not enter into the composition of the fabricated product. Thus, industrial processes that require a large input of energy from raw materials are not likely to locate close to a large market but close to the sources of their raw materials.

## The Rise of Major Metropolitan Areas

Since World War II, the U.S. economy has "matured"; "maturing" is a contemporary metaphor used by economists to signify that the extraction and processing of raw materials come to represent an ever smaller proportion of the value of the national product. Consequently, the advantages that minor metropolitan areas and nonmetropolitan areas enjoyed have become progressively less important over the twenty years between 1950 and 1970.

The population residing in major metropolitan areas has increased from 41 percent in 1950 to 54 percent in 1970, while nonmetropolitan areas have had their share reduced to 30 percent from 42 percent (see Table 1). Minor metropolitan areas have barely maintained their share of the population, dropping slightly from 17 percent of the total to 16 percent. Yet, the index of their per capita income indicates that they have managed to retain industry largely because per capita income has not risen as quickly in minor metropolitan areas as in major metropolitan areas. In 1950, the per capita income of minor metropolitan areas was at 117 percent of the national average. In 1970, it had dropped to the national average. Major metropolitan areas not only increased the proportion of the United States population residing within their boundaries, but they also increased somewhat more rapidly their share of annual

Table 1:   Relative Importance of Places of Residence, 1950 and 1970

|  | Population | | Annual Income | | Index of Income (national average =100) | |
|---|---|---|---|---|---|---|
|  | 1950 | 1970 | 1950 | 1970 | 1950 | 1970 |
|  | Percent of Total | | Percent of Total | | | |
| Major metropolitan | 41% | 54% | 46% | 62% | 112 | 115 |
| Minor metropolitan | 17 | 16 | 20 | 16 | 117 | 100 |
| Nonmetropolitan | 42 | 30 | 34 | 22 | 81 | 73 |

Sources: Bureau of Economic Analysis, Regional Economics Measurement Division; 1950 and 1970 Censuses of Population.

income. Thus, their per capita income rose from 112 percent of the national average in 1950 to 115 percent in 1970.

## Nonmetropolitan America

Minor metropolitan areas have been discussed in relation to major metropolitan areas, and it has been noted that the minor metropolitan sector of the economy is a cross between major metropolitan areas and nonmetropolitan areas. The real contrast to major metropolitan areas is the nonmetropolitan sector of the United States, which can, perhaps, more accurately be labeled the rural and small-town sector (now in the minority not only with respect to wealth but also with respect to numbers).

Rural and small-town America is weak not only because it has become the minority, but also because of an even greater handicap—lack of coordination. Its 64 million inhabitants are spread throughout the more than 2.6 million square miles of the continental United States that are outside of metropolitan areas. This means a population density of about 25 inhabitants per square mile, compared with 600 per square mile in the outskirts of metropolitan areas. Even if one discounts the large stretches of waterless desert and mountain forest contained in this territory, the population density remains so low that distance remains the chief obstacle to all social and economic activity. The simplest way to overcome this obstacle is to locate as closely as possible to one of the arteries of interurban communication. Consequently, there is often better communication between nonmetropolitan and metropolitan America than between the various parts of nonmetropolitan America. The result is that nonmetropolitan America is a reacting, rather than an initiating, sector. Its markets are overseas, or in one or more metropolitan areas; and its tools and consumer goods are channeled to it through metropolitan areas.

The term "urban," as used in the United States Census of Population, refers to the comforts and conveniences made possible by a congregation of inhabitants reaching a size of 2,500. Unfortunately, the boundaries utilized by the Bureau of the Census in defining "urban places" are political. The number of inhabitants in "urban places" is understated because some closely adjoining villages are classified as rural. Nevertheless, these statistics classified 26 million nonmetropolitan inhabitants as residing in "urban places" in 1970. Thus, at least 41 percent of rural and small-town Americans can be classified as small-town, rather than rural; that is, they reside in concentrations of population that have at least 2,500 and fewer than 50,000 inhabitants.

Close examination of historical statistics for nonmetropolitan counties also shows that there has been a steady concentration in small towns throughout several decades of people who had been farmers. As a result, living standards throughout this sector have risen and nonmetropolitan residents are not denied a great share of the needs, or even the luxuries, of metropolitan residents. This is due to the automobile. The great limitation to this potential, of course, is roads, and the primary interest of rural and small-town America has been the construction and maintenance of the roads that facilitate management of the large stretches of territory from which it derives its living. The productivity of this sector has increased very rapidly since 1950, but a necessary condition of this high productivity has been the extensive road-building program of the Federal Government and the states.

The Standard Industrial Code (SIC) is not designed to distinguish between establishments that need to be located in large urban areas and those that are drawn to rural and small-town America. Nevertheless, it does provide some hints as to the reasons why economic activities locate in nonmetropolitan America (see Table 2). One reason, which hardly needs to be documented, is that extractive industries must be located where there are natural resources. Farming and forestry use flat lands and rolling hills. Miners dig or drill wherever metals, fuels, etc., are found. About 14 percent of the nonmetropolitan population works in agriculture, forestry, mining and fisheries (SIC codes 01, 07, 08, 09, 10, 11, 12, 13 and 14) compared with 2 percent of the metropolitan population.

The rural and small-town population is engaged in manufacturing as much as the metropolitan population. Yet, the preponderance of lumber and furniture manufactures (SIC codes 24 and 25) in these areas indicates that manufacturers that process raw materials—such as ore smelters, paper mills, and feed preparers—will often locate at the most convenient point from which they can gather their supplies because they can afford to give less consideration to the problem of shipping to and serving markets. The slight edge in food processing and other nondurable products that nonmetropolitan areas enjoy in terms of the proportion of the labor force engaged in these activities confirms the existence of this factor.

Table 2: Distribution of Metropolitan and Nonmetropolitan Employment, 1970

|  | Percentage of Total Employment | |
|  | Metropolitan | Nonmetropolitan |
| --- | --- | --- |
| Extractive industries[1] | 2% | 14% |
| Construction | 6 | 7 |
| Manufacturing |  |  |
| Textiles | 2 | 5 |
| Lumber products | 1 | 3 |
| Food | 2 | 2 |
| Other nondurables | 3 | 3 |
| Durables (excluding lumber) | 13 | 9 |
| Printing | 2 | 1 |
| Chemical | 1 | 1 |
| Total manufacturing | 24 | 24 |
| Distribution[2] | 10 | 7 |
| Retail and other personal service[3] | 25 | 24 |
| Medical services | 6 | 5 |
| Education services | 8 | 9 |
| "Advanced" services[4] | 13 | 6 |
| Public administration | 6 | 4 |
| Total | 100 | 100 |
| Employment as percent of population | 39% | 35% |

[1] Agriculture, forestry, fisheries and mines.
[2] Rail, trucking, other transport, communications and wholesaling.
[3] Food, bakery, dairy general stores and other stores, eating and drinking places, motor vehicle retail, repair services, household services, entertainment and recreation, utilities and other personal services.
[4] Banking, finance, business, professional, and welfare and nonprofit services.

Sources: U. S. Bureau of the Census and 1970 Census of Population.

A third reason for the location of industries in nonmetropolitan America is indicated by the larger proportion of its labor force engaged in textiles (SIC codes 22 and 23)—an industry that has traditionally relied on a relatively unskilled labor force instead of on a range of diversified skills. Thus, manufacturing that does not require a diversified labor force can be drawn to nonmetropolitan America. A maker of gravestones and statuary, if he employs only stonecutters, could locate near a granite or marble quarry. Economic activity does not find an obstacle to locating in rural and small-town America because it needs a skilled labor force but because it requires *diverse* skills and, therefore, needs to draw on a larger labor market. Indeed, if an industry requires both unskilled and skilled labor, it will do better in meeting its labor requirements by locating within a large metropolitan area where both types of labor may be available. A consequence of having an unskilled labor force is that the employer has one kind of labor; it is this result that enables him to locate in a small town and take advantage of the lower wages that are frequently found there for equivalent skills.

There is much evidence that "home manufacture" and "self-reliance," with the lower standard of living they imply, have nearly disappeared from rural and small-town America. In the first place, the proportion of its population working in organized establishments for a commercial wage appears to be only slightly lower than in metropolitan America, 35 percent of the population compared with 39 percent. But since a smaller proportion of women and a larger proportion of male teenagers work in nonmetropolitan areas, the difference in household self-sufficiency is somewhat understated by this figure. Nevertheless, the days of the self-sufficient country family are gone.

This is also indicated by the fact that contract construction, retailing, personal services, and education occupy much the same proportion of the labor force in nonmetropolitan as in the metropolitan areas. This means that, although there might be some difference in quality or price of what is marketed in nonmetropolitan America which the statistics on employment might not be able to detect, the "hick" has rapidly been disappearing. Outside of poverty areas, rural and small-town America is well-dressed, well-groomed, and well-informed or, at least, roughly on the same level as metropolitan America.

One deficiency occurs with respect to health. The nonmetropolitan resident has fewer medical personnel to serve him on the spot. If he has a complex problem, he has to be referred and transported to a hospital in a major or minor metropolitan area. But the chief deficiency is in the area of "advanced" services. This new term is replacing the older concept of "business and professional" people. A new term is needed because of the proliferation of these callings. The traditional "professions" of clergyman, lawyer, physician, architect, educator and engineer have been joined by such newer ones as management consultant, marketer, social worker, public relations expert, and researcher.

Of course, many of these old and new professions are attached to manufacturing enterprises, distribution organizations, or educational institutions. The SIC code classifies them according to the main purpose of the establishment for which they work. This results in some absurdities, such as the assumed existence of 3,129 "miners" in Manhattan in 1970. On the other hand, an organization providing such "advanced" services may employ many relatively unskilled workers. For example, a commercial bank has more bank tellers than economists. Therefore, the estimated employment provided by these professions is very much of a "guesstimate." Nevertheless, in metropolitan areas organizations providing such advanced services accounted for 13 percent of employment, compared with only 6 percent in nonmetropolitan America.

## Conclusion: The City Mouse and the Country Mouse

Aesop's fable has been handed down over many generations. The country mouse led a simple but secure life. His city cousin enjoyed luxuries, but only by undergoing great risks. The development of the major metropolitan area, however, means that this fable no longer applies, for today major metropolitan areas have a greater economic stability than rural and small-town areas. The city mouse lives in a more stable and predictable market, where there are many alternative jobs and fewer shortages. The country mouse has traded his former self-sufficiency for a higher standard of living, but he resides in an environment that reacts sharply to markets, has a narrow labor market, and often experiences shortages.

As long as the country resident was self-sufficient, while the city lived by trading or by exporting its manufactures to the countryside, the burden of trade fluctuations was felt primarily by the cities. This situation prevailed as late as 1880, but it was to be changed to the present state of affairs (where the major metropolitan area is dominant) by two phases of development: the development of manufacturing from 1880 to 1950, and the new metropolitan phase in which we are at present. These two phases in American economic development are discussed successively in the next two chapters.

# 2.
# The Manufacturing Phase, 1880 to 1950

**"It is necessary to look backwards a little, in order the better to look forwards." (Alfred Marshall, _Industry and Trade,_ 1919)**

THERE HAVE BEEN three phases to the urbanization of the United States. The longest phase began with the settlement of the vast American continent and was over when the Western frontier was declared officially closed by the superintendent of the 1890 Census of Population.[1] The second phase stretched from 1880 to 1950 and coincided with the development of the manufacturing belt north of the Ohio and east of the Mississippi (see Map 1, p. 22). It will be referred to in this chapter as the "manufacturing phase." We are now in the third phase, the "metropolitan phase" of American urbanization (see Chapter 3).

## Prior to 1880

During the first phase, America remained an overwhelmingly agricultural nation but, as each new section became more settled, urban centers rose up to serve the farm population (see Table 3). At that time, American towns and cities were usually trade and transportation centers. The U.S. Bureau of the Census definition of an "urban place" dates from that period. It sets a very low population figure, 2,500 inhabitants, for a place to qualify as "urban." Even using this very low criterion, the United States had only 28 percent of its population in towns and cities in 1880. If one uses the criterion for "metropolitan" adopted for the 1940 Census —a minimum population of 50,000—then only 14 percent of the population was metropolitan in 1880. Only 6 percent of the population resided in areas that had populations of over 500,000.

As late as 1880, the largest cities drew their sustenance from the trade generated by their ports. Except for Chicago and New Orleans, these cities were still located on the Atlantic seaboard, as they had been in

---

[1] See Frederick J. Turner, _The Frontier in American History._ New York: Henry Holt & Co., 1950.

1776, for the bulk of trade in the United States was based on exchanging the raw products of America for the manufactures of Europe. There are certain manufactures, however, that produce a very bulky product, e.g., wagons, or that reduce the bulk of their raw materials (wheat milling, for example). It was mainly these manufactures that held their own against European manufactures, and they usually located close to the agricultural population they served. Thus, in 1880, a large proportion of manufacturing was scattered widely throughout the United States.

The major exception appears to have been New England. Immigrant labor allowed Massachusetts, Rhode Island, and New Hampshire mills to compete with the Europeans in the manufacture of textiles and shoes. In Connecticut, at the same period, there appeared to be a concentration of skilled labor which could produce precision products, such as firearms, as cheaply as the Europeans. In the rest of the United States, however, urban centers were small outside of New York, Philadelphia and Chicago, and their principal manufactures were those that are usually found in transportation centers, e.g., food processing. Rochester, New York, for example, started out in the 19th century as a wheat-milling town. It had a good location on the water routes from the interior to the Atlantic seaboard and plenty of water power with which to grind wheat.

Table 3: United States Urbanization, 1790-1950

| | Towns and Cities with Population | | |
| | Over 2,500 | Over 50,000 | Over 500,000 |
| Census | Percent of Total Population | | |
|---|---|---|---|
| 1790 | 5.1% | — | — |
| 1800 | 6.1 | 2.1% | — |
| 1810 | 7.3 | 2.1 | — |
| 1820 | 7.2 | 2.6 | — |
| 1830 | 8.8 | 3.3 | — |
| 1840 | 10.8 | 4.1 | — |
| 1850 | 15.3 | 6.2 | 2.2% |
| 1860 | 19.8 | 9.8 | 4.4 |
| 1870 | 25.7 | 12.8 | 4.2 |
| 1880 | 28.2 | 14.3 | 6.2 |
| 1890 | 35.1 | 18.6 | 7.1 |
| 1900 | 39.6 | 22.3 | 10.6 |
| 1910 | 45.6 | 26.6 | 12.5 |
| 1920 | 51.2 | n.a. | n.a. |
| 1930 | 56.2 | n.a. | n.a. |
| 1940 | 56.5 | 52.6 | 32.4 |
| 1950 | 64.0 | 54.8 | 37.6 |

n.a.—not available
Sources: 1970 and 1950 Censuses of Population.

**United States Manufacturing Belt, 1937**

MANUFACTURING BELT
(72 Percent of Manufacturing in U.S.A.)

## The Starting Point, 1880

It was the wave of railroad building that started with and followed the Civil War that was to launch the American economy into manufacturing and help to divide it into three major economic sections, the North, the West, and the South. Besides the greater efficiency of the railroads that were built after the Civil War, which made them better transportation arteries than the rivers, roads, and canals that had carried most goods prior to 1880, what happened after the Civil War was that railroads were laid down by the so-called railroad barons according to large strategic plans. Thus, a network of railways suddenly came into place where previously there had been only scattered lines leading from one town to another. As a result, the United States suddenly found that it had a "system" of railways (rather than just a collection), with certain key terminals. Although the United States as a whole found its transportation system vastly improved after the railroad-building era that followed the Civil War, there did develop a very pronounced difference between the ease of transportation in different sections of the nation. East of the Mississippi and North of the Ohio, the railway network was very dense—with many feeder lines and alternate routes. This region of the nation was divided into two sections, the Northeast and the Midwest. The latter section played the role of a balance wheel between the East and the West, but its network of transportation was as good as that of the East. In the South and West, by contrast, the railroads did not come to form a dense network but, rather, long corridors with occasional feeder lines to both sides. As a result, the urbanization of the United States proceeded unevenly. Large cities rose largely in a "manufacturing belt" which was located where the network of railroad transportation was most dense.[2]

## The Growth of Large Cities, 1880-1950

The growth of the American city from 1880 to 1950 coincides largely with the growth of regional and national manufacturing. The 1880 and 1890 Censuses indicate that this growth began some time between 1880 and 1890. In that decade, manufacturing employment in the United States jumped sharply; yet, *local* manufacturing was declining. Manufac-

[2] The "classic" on railroads in 1880 is A. T. Hadley, *Railroad Transportation.* New York: Putnam, 1885. A summary of developments in this period, plus helpful maps of the railroad system in 1880, may be found in D. Philip Locklin, *Economics of Transportation.* Homewood, Ill.: Richard D. Irwin, Inc., 1972, Chapter 6.

turing was becoming concentrated in the North at the hubs of the transportation system.[3] Small towns and cities, with populations of under 50,000, continued to develop as trade centers for a rising population during this period but, due to the fact that they did not attract manufactures, they did not grow as rapidly as cities with populations of over 50,000, for it was manufacturing employment that rose most rapidly during these seventy years from 1880 to 1950.

Between 1880 and 1890, the population residing in cities with more than 50,000 inhabitants jumped sharply from 14 percent to 19 percent of the total population of the United States, starting off a lengthy process of urbanization that was interrupted only in the 1930's by the Depression. By 1950, the rural population had dropped to 36 percent of the total population from 72 percent in 1880; small towns to 9 percent from 14 percent; but 55 percent of the population now resided in cities with populations of over 50,000.

The economic reason for the concentration of manufacturing in large cities was Adam Smith's principle that the "division of labor is limited by the extent of the market." The Northern hubs of the railroad system had access to large regional markets for bulk goods, such as steel, and to national markets for goods with a lower ratio of weight or bulk to price, such as textiles. Due to the division of labor and cost-saving technological advances, large and small manufacturers at the hubs of the transportation system were able to produce manufactured goods more cheaply than local manufacturers. Another important factor that produced a concentration of manufactures was proximity to coal deposits, which were then the principal source of energy for the United States and also the bulkiest ingredient in the production of steel. This explains the difference that developed between the Midwest and the Northeast; while the former tended to specialize in heavy industry, which either required a large input of energy or was based on the production of steel, the latter concentrated on "light," that is, labor-intensive, manufactures.

## Urban Immigration

During the first 34 years of the rise of the large American city (1880-1914), the United States had a policy of unrestricted immigration from

---

[3] See Allan R. Pred, *The Spatial Dynamics of U.S. Urban Industrial Growth.* Cambridge, Mass.: The MIT Press, 1966.

Europe. But the flow of immigration was halted in 1914 by World War I. With the return of peace, European immigrants once again began to arrive. By this time, however, the United States had begun seriously to reconsider its policy of nearly unrestricted immigration, which had been under attack for many years—particularly by labor unions. In 1921, the first Quota Act was passed that reduced immigration to a trickle and it which has been followed by the United States with occasional liberaliza-was followed by another Quota Act in 1924 that confirmed this policy, tions ever since.

Thus, 1914 marked the virtual end of the European immigration into large American cities. From then on, the source for immigrants to the cities became mainly the farms of the United States, where agricultural productivity was rising rapidly. These forces came into full play shortly after the end of World War I. Marginal farmers found that they could not make as good a living from their land as from factory wages. Therefore, they turned to large cities where they could earn more.

Urban political machines had drawn much of their strength from foreign immigration. Thus, halting the flow of the foreign-born into the United States weakened urban political machines. One lasting effect was resistance to annexation by the central city. Prior to 1914, as cities grew and outlying areas were urbanized at a very rapid pace, these were annexed by the central cities. Thereafter, outlying areas began to resist annexation and they were supported by state legislatures, dominated by nonurban legislators—whether from "upstate," as in New York or "downstate," as in Illinois—who sympathized with the desire of these areas to remain politically autonomous. Consequently, annexation came to a virtual halt throughout the North and on the West Coast. The result was that political boundaries and economic boundaries began to diverge widely within urban areas. This "progressive" era laid the seed for the current political structure of most metropolitan areas—many independent governments, ranging from counties to school districts, without an overall government that covers most of the metropolitan area.

## Intraurban Transportation

Although the railroad and steamship had revolutionized interurban transportation by 1880, there had been no important inventions for improving transportation *within* cities and towns, rather than *among* them, as late as 1887. The foot and the hoof were still the two means of transportation available for moving people and goods from one part of an urban area to another. Horse and man cover only about three miles in an hour at a walk. Thus, astronomical land prices and heavy congestion formed a serious barrier to the further development of regional and national manufactures in cities with populations of over 50,000.

This serious bottleneck was broken in part when electric traction was perfected by Frank J. Sprague in 1887, making possible the elevator, the subway and the elevated railroad, and the trolley car. For most cities, the elevator and the trolley were the most important inventions. The elevator enabled merchants and manufacturers to build up where land prices were high. The trolley extended the distance that could be covered by a passenger in an hour to about 15 miles. Therefore, residences and workplaces could be built at a much greater distance from each other and large new areas were opened up for further development. Only a few cities, such as New York, were large enough to install subway systems, which required both a larger service area and higher population densities to become competitive with the trolley. The commuter railroad (supplemented by express trolleys) had a small but crucial importance. It was more expensive, but it enabled those who could afford the fares to reside in the "country" and commute into the city every day for work. It thus brought into being the modern suburb. Previously, the wealthy had sent their families outside the city limits to less urbanized areas in order to escape the summer heat. At the end of the 19th century, however, a part of the wealthier classes began to reside with their families for the whole year outside of the city.

Electric traction was never successfully applied to the problem of moving *goods* within a city. Manufacturers who shipped regionally or nationally could locate in outlying areas connected by railroad spurs to the main lines and railroad yards (or to piers, if they wanted to ship by water). Their labor force could be drawn from many other parts of the city. The daily life of a large city, however, calls for the distribution of many goods through wholesale and retail channels, and the horse and wagon remained the only means of moving these goods until they were replaced by the motorized truck, starting roughly in 1914. Until carting became motorized, horses and wagons continued to contribute heavily to the congestion of American cities.

Furthermore, electric traction brought only a temporary relief of congestion. In order to be efficient, such mass transportation requires stops at fixed locations and a heavy volume of traffic over its routes. Thus, as America's cities continued to grow, land prices rose near the stops of mass transportation facilities, producing strong incentives to build high-density residential areas. Moreover, the trolley and the subway enhanced the value of a central location by making it accessible to the entire city. As a result, much retailing and entertainment became centralized, as did many business services whose customers required accessibility.

Thus, the early 20th century city developed a distinctive outline. Skyscrapers were built to develop a business district in the center. It was usually closely flanked by an entertainment district and a retailing district, the latter dominated by large department stores. Some "light" manufactures, such as apparel, were also located close to the center; some of them required close and frequent contacts with their customers and the elevator enabled them to build up. "Heavy" industry, however, and much "light" industry located on the outskirts, where land was cheap. On the whole, residential districts closer to the center were built up to higher densities.

This pattern was most pronounced in the case of the largest city, New York. In the three cities with important subway or elevated electric railroads—New York, Chicago and Boston—population densities are reported to have risen in some residential districts to as high as 120,000 inhabitants per square mile. There was overcrowding in the poorest sections in five-story, walk-up tenements.[4] In cities with smaller populations, the trolley (and later the bus), which could operate profitably in districts with lower population densities or lower total population, were the common means of intraurban transportation. They were also used in the outlying districts of the largest urbanized areas.

The chief exceptions to the New York pattern were the cities in the South and West, which were smaller, or which, like New Orleans, failed to attract a great deal of manufacturing. Five transportation centers outside of the manufacturing belt developed important manufacturing sectors: San Francisco-Oakland, Los Angeles, Seattle, Minneapolis-St. Paul, and Kansas City, Missouri. They were the principal hubs of the transcontinental railroads, the Southern Pacific, the Union Pacific, and the Great Northern. Nevertheless, these five cities sustained themselves more from trade and transportation than from manufactures, and their chief manufacture was usually the processing of food or the fabrication of farm implements and supplies, i.e., manufactures that tend to locate in transportation centers.

After the restriction of immigration in 1921, the South began to attract more successfully from New England those manufactures (particularly

---

[4] See Juan de Torres, *Economic Dimensions of Major Metropolitan Areas.* National Industrial Conference Board, 1968, for a discussion of the relation between residential densities and types of housing.

textiles) that had relied on cheap labor. These were never drawn into one large center, however, but were scattered along the towns on the route of the Southern Railway from Richmond to Atlanta. Birmingham, despite the close proximity of coal and iron, did not develop as a great industrial center, for it did not enjoy the extensive railway and water connections necessary for a great industrial city to grow up. Thus, the steel centers of the North, such as Pittsburgh, with their greater access to large markets on all sides were able to undercut Birmingham despite the lower wages in the South.[5]

Los Angeles is a unique case, for it launched into the "metropolitan" phase of urbanization some twenty years before this became the prevalent pattern in the United States. As the terminal of two important lines of transportation (from Kansas City and from New Orleans), Los Angeles had started to grow rapidly as early as the turn of the century. From the beginning, Los Angeles adopted a very low-density pattern of development, based on an extensive system of streetcar lines. At the same time, wages were probably higher in Los Angeles than in most of the nation. Thus, when the mass production of lower-priced passenger cars went into full gear in the 1920's, the residents of Los Angeles purchased the most cars per capita in the nation, and started using them for shopping, commuting to work, business calls, and other utilitarian purposes. By 1926, Los Angeles was a "motorized" city, while the cities in the manufacturing belt still relied on mass transportation. Despite the pressures of the Depression and World War II, Los Angeles appears never to have reverted back to mass transportation. It maintained its precedent, later to be followed by nearly every other city in the nation.[6]

## The "City Beautiful" Movement

The rise of the large manufacturing city to prominence in the United States came as a substantial shock to what had been a rural, small-industry economy. Besides the accumulation of large amounts of capital and the growth of mass production, another problem (shared with European nations) stirred American intellectuals, namely, urban ugliness. Although

[5] For the loss of industry in New England see R. C. Eastal, *New England, A Study in Industrial Adjustment*. New York: Frederick A. Praeger, 1966. For the development of the South industrially, see John Samuel Ezell, *The South Since 1865*. London: The Macmillan Company, 1963.

[6] See Robert M. Fogelson, *The Fragmented Metropolis, Los Angeles 1850-1930*. Cambridge, Mass.: Harvard University Press, 1967.

it might be argued that the poor in urban areas enjoyed many more comforts than the early 19th century pioneers, the large urban agglomerations that were growing in the North presented many new problems. As long as factories were small and scattered around the countryside, they generally "melted" into the natural surroundings, and their employees resided where there was plenty of open space in close contact with the farming population. When factories increased in size, however, and became concentrated at a few hubs, an entirely new, man-made environment arose. The links between manufacturing and farming workers were snapped and open space began to become scarce and expensive.

The "City Beautiful" movement was the first attempt in the United States to bring order and beauty to its big, industrial cities. Its principal failure has been probably the "master plan," an attempt to harmonize all land uses within the expected zone of urbanization and even beyond. Since urban growth is not easily predictable, such ambitious plans have usually had to be scrapped or else modified so frequently that they lost any resemblance to the original. The enthusiasm for planning, however, did bring some benefits, largely in the area of transportation planning where a new profession, traffic engineering, arose and helped to bring solutions to the very complex problems that arose in each metropolitan area when its residents began to drive their own cars rather than use mass transportation.[7]

The chief triumph of the "City Beautiful" movement, however, was probably zoning. At first, zoning gave rise to knotty constitutional questions and, in 1917, the Supreme Court struck down a municipal ordinance that had zoned on the basis of race, forbidding blacks to reside in certain sections of the city.[8] Nine years later, however, the Supreme Court approved an ordinance designed to keep manufacturing out of a suburban area and discrimination according to aesthetics was permitted with a limitation in "cases where the general public interest would so far outweigh the interest of the municipality that the municipality would not be allowed to stand in the way."[9] Due to this decision, zoning began to spread and now has become an extensive body of law that varies widely

---

[7] For a balanced estimate of planning efforts, see Joint Center for Urban Studies of the Massachusetts Institute of Technology and Harvard University, *The Effectiveness of Metropolitan Planning*. Washington, D.C.: U.S. Government Printing Office, 1964.

[8] Buchanan V. Warley 245 U.S. 60 (1917).

[9] Village of Euclid V. Ambler Realty Co. 272 U.S. 265 (1926).

from state to state. Other legacies from this era were building codes and fire codes, also administered at the local level.

## Next Steps

By 1929, the United States was on the verge of suburbanization, based on increasingly widespread automobile ownership. Los Angeles was leading the way. But the second phase of urbanization was destined to be prolonged by a depression and a war. From 1930 to 1940, the percentage of the American population residing in urban places with populations of over 2,500 increased only from 56 percent of the total population to 57 percent. World War II brought many young men and women from the farms to work in urban industry, but wartime shortages prevented the manufacture of automobiles and the construction of new housing and new plants. By the 1950 Census of Population, the majority of the population was contained by metropolitan areas, but the population residing in *major* metropolitan areas was still a minority, 38 percent of the total population.

# 3.
# The Metropolitan Phase

THE OUTLINES OF ANYTHING NEW are usually crude and hazy, and in this half-light storytelling flourishes; metropolitan America is no exception. The so-called developed nations are evolving a new form of urban life and are moving away from the old division of the factory worker in the city and the family farm in the country. Indeed, the proportion of the labor force engaged in manufacturing in nonmetropolitan America is as great as that in metropolitan America—24 percent according to the 1970 Census of Population (see Table 2 on page 17).

Luckily, federal statistical agencies have recognized metropolitan areas, and one can draw on the data presented in the 1950, 1960, and 1970 Censuses of Population and Housing. Such data were not available prior to 1950. In addition, annual data are becoming increasingly available. They are often rough estimates, but they enable us to spot new trends much more quickly than we could when only data from the decennial censuses were available. In this chapter, it has been possible to rely much more on statistics than for the earlier period. However, it will probably be some time before the outlines of the new metropolitan area become sufficiently fixed and familiar to allow for more complete accounts of the present phase of urbanization.

## A New Beginning, 1950

There are three principal reasons for marking off post-World War II metropolitan development as a changed process of urbanization. The first is that postwar growth has not been spearheaded by manufacturing but rather by the "service" sector of the economy, a category that includes a wide variety of employments, ranging from soldier to banker. In the 1950 Census, manufacturing employment accounted for 26 percent of total employment in the United States, up from 23 percent in 1940. Between 1950 and 1960, however, manufacturing employment as a percent of total employment dropped slightly to 25 percent and this trend became more pronounced in the next decade when it dropped to 23 percent. Currently, the Bureau of Labor Statistics projects a further fall[1] to slightly below 22

---

[1] Bureau of Labor Statistics, *The U.S. Economy in 1985,* Bulletin 1809. Washington, D.C.: U.S. Government Printing Office, 1974.

percent in 1985. This decline in importance of manufacturing employment has occurred concurrently with a decline in the agricultural labor force from 12 percent of the total in 1950 to 4 percent in 1970.

Thus it is probable that in the postwar period metropolitan growth has tended to be induced by the pull of demand rather than by the development of comparative advantages in the fabrication of goods at strategic points. The growth of the federal budget and of the amount of income that is spent on leisure (whether as recreation or retirement dollars) has been among the chief determinants of where and when metropolitan growth came about. Today, a great deal of income is spent away from where it is earned and, consequently, economic activity must follow it to new markets. Other factors have also had some influence in shifting markets, such as lower wages or a lower cost of living, and possibly an increase in the amount of "footloose" industry.[2] Of course, manufacturing has continued to be an important factor but it does not appear to have been the *chief* factor as was the case prior to 1950.

The second reason for distinguishing the period after World War II is that, as they grew in size, metropolitan areas generally *decreased* in density of population—rather than increased, as had occurred prior to World War II. One of the causes of this trend toward the use of more space is widespread use of the automobile. Passenger-operated transportation became competitive with mass transportation and, in many cases, eliminated it. Of equal importance has been the rise in per capita income. As income rises, people demand not only better and roomier houses but also more land around their dwellings. These developments had a far-reaching effect on the structure of American metropolitan areas.

The third reason for making 1950 a benchmark is a new geographical pattern of urban development, which was to modify substantially the old three-fold division of the United States into the manufacturing North, the West with great natural resources, and the agricultural South (see Table 4). In his famous lectures at the turn of the century, Frederick Jackson Turner had pointed out that, prior to the Civil War, the United States had had a "middle," namely, the border states of Delaware, Maryland and Kentucky, parts of Virginia and Tennessee, and the Southern parts of Ohio, Indiana and Illinois. He forecast that, as the wounds of the Civil War healed, the United States would soon develop a "heartland." The fulfillment of the prediction was long delayed, but developments since

[2] See Benjamin Chinitz, *Freight and the Metropolis*. Cambridge, Mass.: Harvard University Press, 1960.

**Table 4: Population and Employment in Northern, Western and Southern Major Urbanized Areas, 1950 and 1970**

| Region | 1950 | | | 1970 | | |
|---|---|---|---|---|---|---|
| | Population | Employment | Manu-facturing Employment | Population | Employment | Manu-facturing Employment |
| | | | (thousands) | | | |
| North .... | 41,089 | 16,563 | 5,799 | 57,506 | 23,162 | 6,634 |
| West ...... | 12,783 | 5,033 | 1,063 | 26,865 | 10,662 | 2,398 |
| South .... | 4,867 | 1,930 | 359 | 11,048 | 4,384 | 820 |
| Total | 58,739 | 23,526 | 7,221 | 95,419 | 38,208 | 9,852 |

Sources: Tables 5, 6, 7, 9, 10, 11.

World War II are making Turner's prediction at least partially true (see Chapters 4 and 5).

## Regional Characteristics in 1950

Having set forth the three principal reasons for making 1950 a benchmark, one may examine the benchmark itself, that is, the beginnings of the major metropolitan sector as it stands today. There are 29 major metropolitan areas in the old Northern manufacturing belt, 18 in the West, and 13 in the South. Tables 4 and 5 show the very pronounced structure of America's urban sector at this time: the manufacturing belt dominated America's largest urbanized areas, accounting for 70 percent of the large urban population and 80 percent of manufacturing employment. *But* the North itself was heavily influenced by the New York-Northeastern New Jersey urbanized area, which accounted for 31 percent of its population.[3]

## The Urban North in 1950

An urbanized area, as defined by the U.S. Bureau of Census, does not include outskirts that are not urbanized because they have a population density of under 1,000 inhabitants per square mile. A metropolitan area,

---

[3] Note that by including all the present 60 major metropolitan areas, we tend to overstate the importance of the West and the South in the urban economy in 1950. This is the "index number" problem. If one had started with only those areas that were major metropolitan areas in 1950, however, one would understate the importance of what were to become large urban centers. With the benefit of hindsight, however, it is better to use a 1970 base, for it is better adapted for the consideration of current problems.

however, includes these outskirts which often account for 20 percent of the population. Thus, an urbanized area with a population of 400,000 is roughly equal to a metropolitan area with 500,000 inhabitants. On this basis, the North in 1950 had 20 urbanized areas with populations of over 400,000 (see Table 5).

**Table 5: Characteristics of 29 Northern Urbanized Areas, 1950**

| | Population (thousands) | Population Density (inhabitants per square mile) | Total Employment (thousands) | Manufacturing Employment | Manufacturing as Percent of Total |
|---|---|---|---|---|---|
| New York | 12,707 | 9,222 | 5,100 | 1,573 | 30.8% |
| Chicago | 4,921 | 7,713 | 2,144 | 808 | 37.7 |
| Philadelphia-Wilmington | 3,109 | 8,679 | 1,230 | 439 | 35.7 |
| Detroit | 2,659 | 6,734 | 869 | 501 | 57.7 |
| Boston | 2,233 | 6,478 | 868 | 249 | 28.7 |
| Cleveland-Akron | 1,750 | 4,393 | 729 | 307 | 42.1 |
| Pittsburgh | 1,532 | 6,045 | 583 | 222 | 38.1 |
| St. Louis | 1,400 | 6,146 | 576 | 195 | 33.9 |
| Washington | 1,287 | 7,216 | 563 | 42 | 7.5 |
| Baltimore | 1,161 | 7,654 | 472 | 146 | 30.9 |
| Buffalo | 896 | 7,280 | 354 | 145 | 41.0 |
| Milwaukee | 829 | 8,156 | 362 | 155 | 42.8 |
| Cincinnati | 813 | 5,567 | 325 | 109 | 33.5 |
| Providence | 583 | 4,091 | 235 | 106 | 45.1 |
| Indianapolis | 502 | 5,545 | 216 | 48 | 22.2 |
| Louisville | 473 | 7,098 | 190 | 59 | 31.1 |
| Columbus, Ohio | 437 | 6,786 | 177 | 44 | 24.9 |
| Hartford | 424 | 4,290 | 187 | 77 | 41.2 |
| Albany-Schenectady | 416 | 5,780 | 173 | 58 | 33.5 |
| Rochester, N.Y. | 409 | 6,334 | 172 | 78 | 45.3 |
| Toledo | 364 | 5,220 | 148 | 57 | 38.5 |
| Springfield, Mass. | 357 | 2,133 | 146 | 65 | 44.5 |
| Dayton | 347 | 5,541 | 141 | 61 | 43.2 |
| Youngstown-Warren | 298 | 3,778 | 121 | 60 | 49.6 |
| Syracuse | 265 | 6,085 | 110 | 39 | 35.5 |
| New Haven | 245 | 5,232 | 100 | 35 | 35.0 |
| Grand Rapids | 227 | 4,857 | 92 | 37 | 40.2 |
| Allentown-Bethlehem, Pa. | 226 | 4,583 | 95 | 48 | 50.5 |
| Worcester | 219 | 5,031 | 85 | 36 | 42.3 |
| Total | 41,089 | .... | 16,563 | 5,799 | 35.0 |

Source: 1950 Census of Population.

Thus, today's Northern major metropolitan areas were already large in 1950, and the price of land had been driven up, producing high residential densities at their centers. Three urbanized areas, New York, Philadelphia and Milwaukee, had population densities that were higher than 8,000 inhabitants per square mile, and twelve others had population densities that were higher than 6,000 inhabitants per square mile. In general, high population densities were correlated with large size, but there were exceptions like Milwaukee. Thus, this section of the nation entered the automobile age with very large stocks of buildings built on the assumption that *mass* transportation would be the major means of transportation for those who lived or worked there. At the same time, manufacturing was the chief source of employment for nearly every urbanized area in the North.

Only three urbanized areas had a smaller percentage of manufacturing than the national average—Washington, Indianapolis and Columbus. All three had a high proportion of government employment. The dominance of the North by New York, however, was less pronounced in manufacturing than in other urban callings; it accounted for only 27 percent of Northern manufacturing employment compared with 31 percent of total employment in the region. Boston and Baltimore also leaned toward other employments besides manufacturing, although the proportion of their labor force in manufacturing was above the national average, as in the case of New York. The city with the greatest comparative advantage in manufacturing appears to have been Detroit, where the 1950 Census of Population lists 58 percent of employment as manufacturing employment. On the average, manufacturing employment accounted for 35 percent of total employment in the North.

## The Urban West in 1950

In the West, there were 10 urbanized areas in 1950 with populations of over 400,000 in 1950 (see Table 6). The Pacific Coast accounted for 63 percent of these urban residents, due largely to the large size of Los Angeles and San Francisco-Oakland by 1950. Large urbanized areas in the West contained only 28 percent as much population as the large urbanized areas of the North in 1950. The fact that they contained this much was due to Los Angeles, which was the third largest urbanized area in the United States at that time, and to San Francisco-Oakland, which was the seventh largest urbanized area. Together, these two large centers accounted for 54 percent of the population residing in large urbanized areas in the West. Thus, by 1950, the development of the California economy as a separate section of the West was nearly an accomplished fact. San Francisco, the older city, had enlarged on the basis of mass transportation and had a population density of over 6,000 inhabitants per square mile, but Los Angeles had motorized early. Despite its large size, therefore, it had a population density of under 6,000 inhabitants per square mile. All other areas also had low population densities. This provided a distinctive "western" touch to their urban life that was destined to influence the rest of the nation.

Table 6:   Characteristics of 18 Western Urbanized Areas, 1950

| | Population (thousands) | Population Density (inhabitants per square mile) | Total Employment (thousands) | Manufacturing Employment | Manufacturing as Percent of Total |
|---|---|---|---|---|---|
| Los Angeles ....... | 3,996 | 4,587 | 1,564 | 400 | 25.6% |
| San Francisco-Oakland ........ | 2,022 | 7,038 | 795 | 154 | 19.4 |
| Minneapolis-St. Paul. | 985 | 4,265 | 416 | 106 | 25.5 |
| Dallas-Ft. Worth .... | 854 | 3,265 | 371 | 78 | 21.0 |
| Kansas City, Missouri | 698 | 4,687 | 298 | 73 | 24.5 |
| Seattle ........... | 622 | 5,057 | 244 | 48 | 19.7 |
| Portland, Oregon .... | 512 | 4,517 | 205 | 38 | 18.5 |
| Denver ........... | 499 | 4,741 | 196 | 33 | 16.8 |
| San Antonio ........ | 449 | 5,011 | 147 | 17 | 11.6 |
| San Diego ......... | 433 | 3,265 | 133 | 21 | 15.8 |
| Omaha ........... | 310 | 4,666 | 128 | 25 | 19.5 |
| Oklahoma City ...... | 275 | 4,106 | 115 | 13 | 11.3 |
| Salt Lake City ...... | 227 | 2,988 | 85 | 12 | 14.1 |
| Phoenix ........... | 216 | 3,921 | 73 | 8 | 11.0 |
| Sacramento ....... | 212 | 5,091 | 85 | 9 | 10.6 |
| Tulsa ............. | 206 | 5,472 | 86 | 16 | 18.6 |
| San Bernardino ..... | 136 | 2,244 | 44 | 5 | 11.4 |
| Fresno ............ | 131 | 4,282 | 48 | 7 | 14.6 |
| Total ....... | 12,783 | .... | 5,033 | 1,063 | 21.1 |

Source: 1950 Census of Population.

With the exception of San Francisco, this section of the nation did not enter the era of passenger-operated transportation with a stock of buildings planned on the basis of utilizing mass transportation. One may also note the relative unimportance of manufacturing in this section of the nation. In 1950, there were only 1,063,000 manufacturing employees in the West, that is, 18 percent of the number employed in the manufacturing North. Of these, 400,000 (about 40 percent) were concentrated in Los Angeles. On the average, in these 18 future major metropolitan areas, manufacturing employment accounted for only 21 percent of employment, compared with the national average of 26 percent.

# The Urban South in 1950

Of the three traditional regions of the United States, the agricultural South was furthest behind with respect to urbanization. At present, the South has 13 major metropolitan areas but, in 1950, it had only 6, and the largest one, Houston, was 18th in size in the United States and located in the Western portion. The total population residing in today's Southern major metropolitan areas in 1950 was only 12 percent as great as that of the North. Manufacturing was less developed even in large cities. Among urbanized areas with populations of over 400,000, only Birmingham had a higher proportion of its employment engaged in manufacturing than the national average. And yet, in the "Pittsburgh of the South" there were only 45,000 manufacturing employees compared with 307,000 in Pittsburgh itself.

Table 7:  Characteristics of 13 Southern Urbanized Areas, 1950

| | Population (thousands) | Population Density (inhabitants per square mile) | Total Employment (thousands) | Manufacturing Employment | Manufacturing as Percent of Total |
|---|---|---|---|---|---|
| Houston | 701 | 2,594 | 290 | 62 | 21.3% |
| New Orleans | 660 | 6,406 | 247 | 38 | 15.4 |
| Atlanta | 508 | 4,814 | 215 | 39 | 18.1 |
| Miami | 459 | 3,937 | 187 | 15 | 8.0 |
| Birmingham | 445 | 4,431 | 169 | 45 | 26.6 |
| Memphis | 406 | 3,705 | 170 | 35 | 20.6 |
| Norfolk-Portsmouth | 385 | 6,172 | 121 | 20 | 16.5 |
| Tampa-St. Petersburg | 294 | 2,658 | 106 | 16 | 15.1 |
| Nashville | 259 | 4,821 | 107 | 24 | 22.4 |
| Richmond | 258 | 5,330 | 114 | 25 | 21.9 |
| Jacksonville | 243 | 4,782 | 98 | 12 | 12.2 |
| Greensboro-Winston-Salem | 176 | 3,734 | 77 | 26 | 33.8 |
| Orlando | 73 | 2,938 | 29 | 2 | 6.9 |
| Total | 4,867 | .... | 1,930 | 359 | 18.6 |

Source: 1950 Census of Population.

Altogether, there were 359,000 manufacturing employees in the South in what were to be its major metropolitan areas compared with 5,799,000 in the North. Consequently, manufacturing employment in these areas came to only 6 percent of that of the North. The chief reason was probably that manufacturing had been drawn by low wages rather than great markets. Manufacturing in large urban areas in the South did not flourish prior to 1950.

37

Thus, postwar metropolitan growth started from very different bases. In the North, there was a sizable inheritance from the period of growth that stretched from 1880 to 1950. Fourteen urbanized areas had population densities of over 6,000 inhabitants per square mile, and manufacturing dominated the economies of nearly every urbanized area. In the West, the foundations had been laid for the heavy urbanization of California's economy that was to follow World War II. Only one city however, had a population density higher than 6,000 inhabitants per square mile, San Francisco-Oakland. The West as a whole had enjoyed both high wages and rapid growth for many years prior to 1950 relative to the rest of the nation, and thus its cities were much newer than those of the older sections of the nation. In the South, finally, there was hardly anything to start from besides Houston, New Orleans, and Atlanta, three important transportation centers. Manufacturing practically had to start from scratch. With the exception of Birmingham and of the small mill towns in the Piedmont region, most Southern cities were small trading and transportation centers servicing a still predominantly agricultural population. Miami was an exceptional case of a city built on vacation and retirement dollars.

## Overall Postwar Progress

In order to keep in view the point of departure, the traditional division into North, South and West will be maintained in this chapter. The new geographic configuration that is arising will be presented in Chapters 4 and 5. By adhering to the lines of this traditional division, the forces that have been at work to break down the old economic barriers between these regions become more readily apparent. World War II, as has been indicated, brought a resumption of the migration from rural to metropolitan areas that had been interrupted during the Depression. The metropolitan population grew at roughly 2.3 percent per annum in the 1940-1950 decade. The rate of increase accelerated in the decade of the 1950's to 3.2 percent per annum, and then declined to 2.2 percent per annum from 1960 to 1970.[4]

There are three sources of metropolitan growth. The first is the natural increase of the population, which was high from 1950 to 1960. Natural

[4] The introduction of "metropolitan districts" in 1940 and "metropolitan areas" in 1950 by the Bureau of the Census makes reliable statistics available for the period after 1940. The 1950-1960 decade showed a high rate of increase not only due to migration but also to a pronounced rise in the birthrate.

increase has two effects, an immediate one as households expand and begin to spend resources to raise their children and a more remote one occurring from 16 to 25 years later as the children grow up, enter the labor force, and begin to establish their own households. In the United States, however, the mobility of the population is very high and it reaches a peak when individuals are entering, or have just entered, the labor force, that is, in the late teens and early twenties. The second effect, therefore, does not need to correspond with the natural increase of a major metropolitan area because the children may decide to go elsewhere.[5]

Table 8: Proportions of North, West and South Major Urbanized Areas, 1950 and 1970

| Region | 1950 | | | 1970 | | |
|---|---|---|---|---|---|---|
| | Population | Employment | Manufac-turing Employment | Population | Employment | Manufac-turing Employment |
| | Percent of Total | | | | | |
| North . . . . . . . | 70.0 | 70.4 | 80.3 | 60.2 | 60.6 | 69.2 |
| West . . . . . . . | 21.8 | 21.4 | 14.7 | 28.2 | 27.9 | 24.3 |
| South . . . . . . . | 8.3 | 8.2 | 5.0 | 11.6 | 11.5 | 8.3 |
| | (thousands) | | | | | |
| Total . . | 58,739 | 23,526 | 7,221 | 95,419 | 38,208 | 9,852 |

Source: Table 4.

The second source of metropolitan growth is migration, from rural areas or from other metropolitan areas. Until 1950, migration consisted largely of young men and women looking for higher wages. In the post-war world, as a result of sharp increases in retirement benefits from both governmental and private pension funds, the migration of retired persons has gained greatly in importance.

The third source of growth is sometimes overlooked because, in a sense, it is not growth but consolidation. It is a combination of the two and can be called "conurbation," the process whereby two or more urbanized areas, by extending their transportation facilities and their urbanized land, eventually melt into each other. Thus, the Miami area now forms one large whole, with a dominant center at Miami, comprising about

[5] The "rootlessness" of America's youth makes for very efficient labor markets, for stagnation in one area is counterbalanced by readiness to emigrate. But it may also have "social costs." See Vance Packard, *A Nation of Strangers*. New York: David Mackay Company, Inc., 1972.

2,122,000 inhabitants in 1970 compared to only 459,000 in 1950 centered around Miami. Growth has fanned out not only from Miami, but from Fort Lauderdale and West Palm Beach to the north, until these three nuclei formed a continuous whole by 1970. This process has also occurred on a large scale between 1950 and 1970 in San Francisco-San Jose, Philadelphia-Wilmington, Boston, Cleveland-Akron, Bridgeport-New Haven, Seattle-Tacoma, Norfolk-Newport News, and San Bernardino-Riverside. It has occurred on a smaller scale in most other urbanized areas because of the great expansion of roads that followed World War II and the low-density suburban developments that often surrounded what had been isolated towns standing on their outskirts.

On the whole, the urban population in today's major metropolitan areas grew at an average rate of 2.5 percent annually from 1950 to 1970 but manufacturing employment grew only at 1.6 percent. Given that the North was the manufacturing center of the nation, one would expect slower population growth in the North than in the West and South. This is what occurred, and certainly it may be argued that, if manufacturing employment had grown more rapidly, the North would have grown more rapidly in population than it did.

But the slower growth of manufacturing employment does not give a complete account of what occurred from 1950 to 1970. During this period there was a very sharp differential between the rates of growth of manufacturing employment in the North, West and South. In the North, manufacturing employment grew 0.7 percent annually, but in the West and the South growth was 4.2 percent. Consequently, the share of the urbanized population residing in major metropolitan areas in the North dropped from 70 percent in 1950 to 60 percent in 1970, and there was a concurrent loss in its share of manufacturing employment from 80 percent to 69 percent.

## Urban Change in the North

Both of these factors, the slow growth of manufacturing employment nationally and its sharply slower growth in the old manufacturing belt, have wrought a sharp change in the economies of Northern cities. In 26 out of 29 Northern major metropolitan areas, manufacturing employment as a percentage of total employment has fallen—often very sharply—from its 1950 level. It has risen only in Indianapolis, Louisville and Bridgeport-New Haven. Of course, part of this drop can be attributed to the dispersion of factory workers beyond even the newly urbanized areas, but most

## Table 9:  Characteristics of 29 Northern Urbanized Areas, 1970

| | Population (thousands) | Population Density (inhabitants per square mile) | Total Employment (thousands) | Manufac- turing Employment | Manufacturing as Percent of Total |
|---|---|---|---|---|---|
| New York | 16,206 | 6,683 | 6,528 | 1,602 | 24.5% |
| Chicago | 6,715 | 5,257 | 2,733 | 880 | 32.2 |
| Philadelphia-Wilmington | 4,392 | 5,101 | 1,725 | 514 | 29.8 |
| Detroit | 3,971 | 4,533 | 1,492 | 557 | 37.3 |
| Boston | 3,185 | 3,226 | 1,316 | 327 | 24.8 |
| Cleveland-Akron | 2,694 | 2,816 | 1,069 | 391 | 36.6 |
| Washington | 2,481 | 5,018 | 1,048 | 66 | 6.3 |
| St. Louis | 1,883 | 4,088 | 898 | 259 | 28.8 |
| Pittsburgh | 1,846 | 3,095 | 680 | 204 | 30.0 |
| Baltimore | 1,580 | 5,103 | 635 | 169 | 26.6 |
| Milwaukee | 1,252 | 2,744 | 514 | 179 | 34.8 |
| Cincinnati-Hamilton | 1,201 | 3,230 | 460 | 147 | 32.0 |
| Buffalo | 1,087 | 5,085 | 415 | 136 | 32.8 |
| Indianapolis | 820 | 2,152 | 332 | 93 | 28.0 |
| Providence | 795 | 3,258 | 327 | 126 | 38.5 |
| Columbus, Ohio | 790 | 3,369 | 321 | 73 | 22.7 |
| Bridgeport-New Haven | 761 | 2,966 | 321 | 115 | 35.8 |
| Louisville | 739 | 3,514 | 289 | 95 | 32.9 |
| Rochester, N.Y. | 601 | 4,127 | 248 | 99 | 39.9 |
| Dayton | 686 | 3,060 | 267 | 102 | 38.2 |
| Hartford | 596 | 3,590 | 262 | 83 | 31.7 |
| Springfield, Mass. | 514 | 2,163 | 202 | 69 | 34.2 |
| Toledo | 488 | 2,947 | 191 | 63 | 33.0 |
| Albany-Schenectady | 487 | 3,233 | 198 | 42 | 21.2 |
| Youngstown-Warren | 396 | 3,076 | 148 | 61 | 41.2 |
| Syracuse | 376 | 3,910 | 149 | 40 | 26.8 |
| Allentown-Bethlehem, Pa. | 364 | 3,691 | 154 | 69 | 44.8 |
| Grand Rapids | 353 | 2,412 | 135 | 42 | 31.1 |
| Worcester | 247 | 2,931 | 101 | 31 | 30.7 |
| Total | 57,506 | .... | 23,162 | 6,634 | 28.6 |

Source: 1970 Census of Population.

of it corresponds to a sharp drop in the importance of manufacturing in the economic life of Northern cities.

The postwar growth of Northern cities was induced by the development of new economic functions outside of manufacturing. Thus, they managed to grow at 1.7 percent annually during this period despite the fact that manufacturing employment was increasing at only 0.7 percent. Northern cities have departed substantially in the postwar period from the old form that used to constitute the American city, namely, a large agglomeration of factories, usually specializing in one branch of manufactures. There remain some urbanized areas that are heavily specialized in manufacturing (though not as much as in 1950): Allentown-Bethlehem, Pa. (45 percent of employment in 1970); Youngstown-Warren, Ohio (41 percent); Rochester, N.Y. (40.0 percent); Providence, R.I. (39 percent); Dayton, Ohio (38 percent), and Detroit (37 percent). With the exception of Detroit, however, most of these urbanized areas are relatively small. As Northern cities increase in size, their dependence on manufacturing lessens. The average proportion of manufacturing employment to total employment in the North is now 29 percent, instead of 35 percent as it was in 1950. This is only 21 percent above the national average; in 1950 it was 35 percent above the national average, which had declined in the 20 years since 1950.

## Urban Change in the West

In the West, the growth of urbanized areas has been much more rapid, 3.8 percent annually, compared with 1.7 percent for the North. Consequently, the West's share of the urbanized population in major metropolitan areas has increased from 22 percent in 1950 to 28 percent in 1970. But, in contrast to the North, the growth of manufacturing has been outpacing the growth of other types of employment. Manufacturing employment in Western cities grew at 4.2 percent per annum, outstripping the growth in population.

Most of this growth in manufacturing was concentrated in Los Angeles, which at present is second to New York in the size of its manufacturing sector and has a greater share of its labor force engaged in manufacturing than New York (28 percent as against 25 percent). Nevertheless, this pattern was also followed by most other Western urbanized areas. Thirteen out of 18 increased the proportion of their employment in manufacturing. As a result, manufacturing now accounts for the same proportion of employment in the West as it does nationally, that is, 23 percent. Thus, Western and Northern urbanized areas have come to resemble each other more closely.

In 1950, Western urbanized areas were mainly trade and transportation centers that manufactured mainly as a service to the vast regions they served; by 1970, they had developed important manufacturing centers that could stand on their own and compete with other centers of manufacturing for markets outside of their own immediate regions. This is particularly true of the five largest manufacturing centers, Los Angeles

**Table 10: Characteristics of 18 Western Urbanized Areas, 1970**

| | Population (thousands) | Population Density (inhabitants per square mile) | Total Employment (thousands) | Manufac- turing Employment | Manufacturing as Percent of Total |
|---|---|---|---|---|---|
| Los Angeles | 8,351 | 5,313 | 3,340 | 925 | 27.7% |
| San Francisco-San Jose | 4,013 | 4,188 | 1,621 | 326 | 20.1 |
| Dallas-Ft. Worth | 2,016 | 1,884 | 858 | 222 | 25.9 |
| Minneapolis-St. Paul | 1,704 | 2,363 | 721 | 177 | 24.5 |
| Seattle-Tacoma | 1,571 | 3,010 | 592 | 134 | 22.6 |
| San Diego | 1,198 | 3,148 | 384 | 68 | 17.7 |
| Kansas City, Missouri | 1,102 | 2,234 | 521 | 118 | 22.6 |
| Denver | 1,047 | 3,577 | 422 | 70 | 16.6 |
| Phoenix | 863 | 2,228 | 331 | 68 | 20.5 |
| Portland, Oregon | 825 | 3,092 | 333 | 66 | 19.8 |
| San Antonio | 772 | 3,466 | 248 | 29 | 11.7 |
| Sacramento | 634 | 2,595 | 231 | 21 | 9.1 |
| San Bernardino-Riverside | 584 | 1,884 | 196 | 37 | 18.9 |
| Oklahoma City | 580 | 1,710 | 240 | 33 | 13.8 |
| Omaha | 492 | 3,252 | 189 | 33 | 17.5 |
| Salt Lake City | 479 | 2,601 | 191* | 30* | 15.7 |
| Tulsa | 371 | 2,063 | 151 | 30 | 19.9 |
| Fresno | 263 | 3,324 | 93 | 11 | 11.8 |
| Total | 26,865 | .... | 10,662 | 2,398 | 22.5 |

*Data for SMSA from Bureau of Labor Statistics; 1950 SMSA base is 100 and 14.
Source: 1970 Census of Population.

(manufacturing employment of 925,000), San Francisco-San Jose (326,-000), Dallas-Ft. Worth (222,000), Minneapolis-St. Paul (177,000), and Seattle-Tacoma (134,000).

## Urban Change in the South

The thirteen Southern major metropolitan areas have experienced even more rapid population growth than Western major metropolitan areas, 4.0 percent annually. Urbanization, however, started from a very low base, and consequently they account for only 12 percent of the urbanized population in major metropolitan areas in 1970 (compared with 8 percent in 1950). Furthermore, although much has been made of the "industrialization" of the South, manufacturing employment is still below average, accounting for 19 percent of total employment in 1970—unchanged from 1950.

Unlike their Northern and Western neighbors, these major metropolitan areas have not experienced great change in the structure of their labor force during the last twenty years. However, since the national average for manufacturing employment's share of total employment has declined to 23 percent, Southern major metropolitan areas no longer fall as far below the national norm as they did in 1950. Furthermore, deviation from the national norm occurs mainly in five cases that pull the average down—the four Florida major metropolitan areas, Miami (14 percent), Tampa-St. Petersburg (15 percent), Jacksonville (12 percent), Orlando (14 percent)—and New Orleans (14 percent). One major metropolitan area, Greensboro - Winston-Salem (43 percent) is far above the national average and can be ranked with manufacturing metropolitan areas in the North. The remaining seven major metropolitan areas are all close to the national average; Houston, with 20 percent of its employment in manufacturing, has the most important manufacturing sector, 138,000 workers and it is rivaled by Miami with 119,000 workers.

Table 11:   Characteristics of 13 Southern Urbanized Areas, 1970

| | Population (thousands) | Population Density (inhabitants per square mile) | Total Employment (thousands) | Manufac- turing Employment | Manufacturing as Percent of Total |
|---|---|---|---|---|---|
| Miami | 2,122 | 3,494 | 874 | 119 | 13.6% |
| Houston | 1,679 | 3,115 | 689 | 138 | 20.0 |
| Atlanta | 1,173 | 2,696 | 501 | 92 | 18.4 |
| New Orleans | 962 | 5,227 | 343 | 47 | 13.7 |
| Norfolk- Newport News | 937 | 2,120 | 289 | 52 | 18.0 |
| Tampa-St. Petersburg | 864 | 2,969 | 293 | 44 | 15.0 |
| Memphis | 664 | 3,396 | 253 | 52 | 20.6 |
| Birmingham | 558 | 2,485 | 208 | 48 | 23.1 |
| Jacksonville | 530 | 1,508 | 192 | 23 | 12.0 |
| Nashville | 448 | 1,306 | 184 | 39 | 21.2 |
| Richmond | 417 | 2,881 | 179 | 36 | 20.1 |
| Greensboro - Winston-Salem | 389 | 2,170 | 267 | 114* | 42.7 |
| Orlando | 305 | 2,320 | 112 | 16 | 14.3 |
| Total | 11,048 | . . . . | 4,384 | 820 | 18.7 |

*Data for SMSA from Bureau of Labor Statistics; 1950 SMSA base is 145 and 57.

Source: 1970 Census of Population.

Thus, while manufacturing employment in the South accounts for only 8 percent of total manufacturing employment in major metropolitan areas, a fairly important base has been built up which provides some competition to Northern major metropolitan areas. The South can now draw manufacturing not only to small towns, where wages and the cost of living are low, but also to such larger centers as Miami, Houston, Atlanta and Greensboro - Winston-Salem.

## The Results in 1970

It has already been pointed out that the whole drift of postwar metropolitan growth has been to place the majority of the American population in the new environment of *major* metropolitan areas with their large markets. But the growth of major metropolitan areas has probably ameliorated the traditional rifts in the nation between North and South before the Civil War, and East and West during the post-Civil War period of rapid industrialization.

Urban growth has been far more rapid in the West and in the South than in the North. Thus, while the North maintains its lead in the number of large cities that it contains, this lead is no longer as pronounced as it was in 1950. In fact, the second largest urbanized area is now Los Angeles, replacing Chicago. Indeed, the California economy is now as highly urbanized as any other section of the nation. The outlines of the manufacturing belt have become blurred. While it is true that most major metropolitan areas in the manufacturing belt have a higher proportion of employment in manufacturing than those in the West and the South, manufacturing employment in these urbanized areas was only 14 percent higher in 1970 than in 1950. In the West, it had increased by 126 percent from a base of 1,063,000 in 1950, and it had increased by 127 percent in the South from a base of 359,000 in 1950.

Much of the decline in this difference may be attributed to the declining importance of water and railroad transportation in the American economy and the rise of over-the-road transportation, although a large part can also be attributed to the extension of better transportation to all parts of the nation. A federal program to help states build roads had been started as early as 1916, but it did not reach massive proportions until the Federal Government began to commit large funds to build the Interstate Highway System in 1956. The construction of the Interstate Highway System has accelerated trends which were under way prior to 1950, but were proceeding at a much slower rate.[6]

[6] For the history of federal aid to highways, see Michael Levy and Juan de Torres, *Federal Revenue Sharing with the States.* The Conference Board, 1970, Report No. 114.

The motor age and the development of roads also lowered population densities within urbanized areas in major metropolitan areas. From 1880 to 1950, cities generally increased their population densities as they grew in size, but after 1950 increased size coincided in nearly all cases with decreasing population densities. Earlier, as a city grew, site values in the center rose in price. The original buildings were then torn down and replaced by buildings that housed more families per acre of land (or were converted to commercial use). But widespread ownership of automobiles after World War II, together with new roads, opened up vast new areas that competed with land in the old urbanized areas and kept its price down. Thus, one powerful incentive to build upward was removed.

**Table 12: Major Urbanized Areas, Frequency Distribution of Population Densities, 1950 and 1970**

| Inhabitants per square mile | North 1950 | North 1970 | West 1950 | West 1970 | South 1950 | South 1970 | United States 1950 | United States 1970 |
|---|---|---|---|---|---|---|---|---|
| 8,000-9,999 | 3 | 0 | 0 | 0 | 0 | 0 | 3 | 0 |
| 6,000-7,999 | 12 | 1 | 1 | 0 | 2 | 0 | 15 | 1 |
| 4,000-5,999 | 13 | 8 | 12 | 2 | 5 | 1 | 30 | 11 |
| 2,000-3,999 | 1 | 20 | 5 | 13 | 7 | 10 | 13 | 43 |
| 0-2,000 | 0 | 0 | 0 | 3 | 0 | 2 | 0 | 5 |

Sources: Tables 5, 6, 7, 9, 10, 11.

In 1950, 30 urbanized areas in today's major metropolitan areas had population densities of 4,000-5,999 inhabitants per square mile and 15 were in the 6,000 to 7,999 range (see Table 12). In 1970, nearly all urbanized areas—43 out of 60—were in the 2,000 to 3,999 range. The median of population density has shifted downward despite the fact that all these urbanized areas were substantially larger in 1970 than in 1950.

## Current Trends

Two current trends in metropolitan America are likely to persist into the future. The first is the slowing of *net* migration into major metropolitan areas to the point where it has approached zero according to the latest (1970-1973) statistics on net migration (see Table 13). The second is the continuing shift in population away from the old manufacturing belt, particularly to the South.

In 1960-1965, there was already evidence that the high rate of migra-

**Table 13: Annual Rates of Major Metropolitan Growth, 1970-1973**

| | Total Change | Natural Increase | Net Migration |
|---|---|---|---|
| Orlando | +6.2 | +0.9 | +5.3 |
| Tampa-St. Petersburg | +5.3 | 0.0 | +5.3 |
| Phoenix | +5.0 | +1.3 | +3.7 |
| Miami SCA | +4.0 | +0.4 | +3.6 |
| Denver-Boulder | +3.4 | +1.1 | +2.3 |
| Atlanta | +2.8 | +1.3 | +1.5 |
| San Diego | +2.8 | +1.0 | +1.8 |
| Sacramento | +2.6 | +0.8 | +1.8 |
| San Antonio | +2.5 | +1.5 | +1.0 |
| Honolulu | +2.5 | +1.7 | +0.8 |
| Omaha | +2.4 | +1.1 | +1.3 |
| Salt Lake City | +2.3 | +1.9 | +0.4 |
| Houston | +2.3 | +1.5 | +0.8 |
| Oklahoma City | +2.3 | +1.1 | +1.2 |
| Portland, Oregon | +1.9 | +0.6 | +1.3 |
| Jacksonville | +1.9 | +1.1 | +0.8 |
| Nashville | +1.8 | +0.9 | +0.9 |
| Charlotte-Gastonia | +1.6 | +1.2 | +0.4 |
| Washington, D.C. | +1.5 | +1.1 | +0.4 |
| San Bernardino-Riverside | +1.5 | +0.9 | +0.6 |
| Greensboro-Winston-Salem | +1.4 | +0.9 | +0.5 |
| Fresno | +1.3 | +1.0 | +0.3 |
| Columbus, Ohio | +1.3 | +1.1 | +0.2 |
| Memphis | +1.2 | +1.1 | +0.1 |
| Tulsa | +1.1 | +0.9 | +0.2 |
| Albany-Schenectady | +0.9 | +0.5 | +0.4 |
| San Francisco-San Jose SCA | +0.9 | +0.7 | +0.2 |
| Dallas-Ft. Worth | +0.9 | +1.2 | -0.3 |
| Indianapolis | +0.8 | +1.1 | -0.3 |
| Richmond | +0.8 | +0.7 | +0.1 |

| (continued) | Total Change | Natural Increase | Net Migration |
|---|---|---|---|
| Allentown-Bethlehem, Pa. | +0.8 | +0.3 | +0.5 |
| Toledo | +0.8 | +0.9 | -0.1 |
| Baltimore | +0.7 | +0.6 | +0.1 |
| Louisville | +0.7 | +0.9 | -0.2 |
| Birmingham | +0.7 | +0.8 | -0.1 |
| Springfield, Mass. | +0.7 | +0.6 | +0.1 |
| Boston SCA | +0.7 | +0.6 | +0.1 |
| Milwaukee | +0.7 | +0.8 | -0.1 |
| Grand Rapids | +0.6 | +0.9 | -0.3 |
| Worcester | +0.6 | +0.5 | +0.1 |
| Kansas City, Missouri | +0.5 | +0.9 | -0.4 |
| New Haven | +0.5 | +0.6 | -0.1 |
| Norfolk-Newport News | +0.5 | +1.2 | -0.7 |
| Providence | +0.5 | +0.4 | +0.1 |
| Youngstown-Warren | +0.5 | +0.7 | -0.2 |
| Minneapolis-St. Paul | +0.5 | +1.0 | -0.5 |
| Chicago SCA | +0.3 | +1.1 | -0.8 |
| Hartford | +0.3 | +0.7 | -0.4 |
| Los Angeles SCA | +0.2 | +0.9 | -0.7 |
| Syracuse | +0.2 | +0.8 | -0.6 |
| Cincinnati-Hamilton SCA | +0.2 | +0.9 | -0.7 |
| Detroit | +0.1 | +1.0 | -0.9 |
| Philadelphia-Wilmington SCA | +0.1 | +0.6 | -0.5 |
| Buffalo | +0.1 | +0.5 | -0.4 |
| Rochester, N.Y. | +0.1 | +0.8 | -0.7 |
| Dayton | -0.1 | +1.0 | -1.1 |
| New York SCA | -0.1 | +0.5 | -0.6 |
| St. Louis | -0.3 | +0.8 | -1.1 |
| Pittsburgh | -0.5 | +0.3 | -0.8 |
| Cleveland-Akron SCA | -0.7 | +0.6 | -1.3 |

Source: U.S. Bureau of the Census, Current Population Reports, No. 537, December, 1974, p. 25.

tion of the 1950's from rural areas into large urbanized areas had declined substantially.[7] The cause of this slowdown was the dwindling share of the total population accounted for by the farm population. By 1970, the farm population was down to 10 million, while the major metropolitan sector was at roughly 110 million. Thus, even if past rates of decrease in the farm population are maintained, the base from which they are deducted has now become so small and the base to which they are to be added has become so great that net migration from rural areas to major metropolitan areas is likely to have very little influence on the growth of the latter.

It is also important to note that, in 1973, the tendency of farm income to decline as a share of national income (continued since 1948) was sharply interrupted. This particular postwar trend can no longer be extrapolated mechanically into the future. Some experts believe that sizable food and natural fiber shortages are developing in the world. If prices for these products stay high and the United States adopts a policy of promoting agricultural exports, then there might be a reversal of past trends. Thus, in the immediate future, by far the largest part of all migration (unless the United States radically changes its policies with respect to immigration from abroad) will be intermetropolitan migration, that is, the increase in size of certain metropolitan areas will come from the decrease of others. Thus, any gain in population for the metropolitan sector as a whole will have to come for the most part from natural increase, that is, the excess of births over deaths.

In 1970-1973, the median annual rate of change in population for the major metropolitan sector was 0.8 percent (down from 2.2 percent in 1960-1970) and the median of net migration over the three years in question was zero. But the second trend mentioned above—the shift of the population away from the old manufacturing belt—meant that most major metropolitan areas falling below the median were located in the North. Thus, the five major metropolitan areas that actually lost population from 1970 to 1973 were all located in the former manufacturing belt. They are the Cleveland-Akron SCA, Pittsburgh, St. Louis, the New York SCA, and Dayton. The five highest rates of increase, on the other hand, are found in the West and the South. They are Orlando, Tampa-St. Petersburg, Phoenix, the Miami SCA, and Denver-Boulder.

---

[7] See Appendix Tables in Juan de Torres, *Economic Dimensions of Major Metropolitan Areas*. The Conference Board, 1968, TP 18. For the situation in the 1950's, see Edward C. Banfield and Morton Grodzins, *Government and Housing in Major Metropolitan Areas*. New York: McGraw-Hill Book Co., 1958.

Another significant trend is signaled by the fact that the Los Angeles SCA, which had experienced a very high flow of immigration throughout a very long stretch of time, experienced a relatively high rate of *emigration* from 1970 to 1973, about 0.7 percent yearly. In general, the smaller major metropolitan areas are experiencing immigration and the larger ones are experiencing emigration. This phenomenon cannot be completely separated from the fact that, for the most part, the smaller major metropolitan areas are located in the South and West. Yet it does bear a simple explanation of its own, namely, that many of the advantages of major metropolitan areas begin to be offset by substantial disadvantages as they grow in size. Thus, the breakdown of the old division into North, West and South is likely to continue in the foreseeable future, leading to the new configuration of economic regions that is described below. At the same time, the larger major metropolitan areas are likely to lose part of their share of the entire population residing in major metropolitan areas.

# 4.
# The American Rimland

*"The difference between philosophy and gossip is only the difference between realizing the part as a part of the whole and looking at it in its isolation as if it really stood apart." (Oliver Wendell Holmes)*

IT IS IMPORTANT to place each major metropolitan area in the context of the national economy. This means that one can no longer use the traditional three-way split of the United States into a North, West and South. The last twenty-five years, as shown in the preceding chapter, have greatly modified the traditional barriers that had arisen from the Civil War and the urbanization of the North. Thus, the new geographical elements of the economic life of America are substantially different now from what they were in 1932—or even as late as 1948. Aside from the growing resemblance among major metropolitan areas and the more rapid extension of urbanization outside of the North, there are two additional significant developments: the growth of a highly urbanized region within California and the political end of the "Solid South."[1] The result is a highly complex configuration that is evolving towards a form that is common to many other nations, namely, a "heartland" and a "rimland," geographical names that correspond roughly to the notion of a middle and its extremes. This was the form that characterized the early days of American history when there existed a "Border Region" including such states as Pennsylvania, Maryland, and Virginia.

In order to place each major metropolitan area in its context, the United States economy has been divided into twelve regions following the outline in nearly all cases of the main axes of transportation. In order to catch the new economic reality, six regions have been placed in the "rimland" and six in the "heartland." The present chapter will deal with the six regions comprising the "rimland," and the next chapter with the six comprising the "heartland."

---

[1] It is always difficult to date a state of mind such as that of the "Solid South." It is probable, however, that this persistent feature of American civilization started with the Mexican-American War of 1846 and did not end until 1948 when the Dixiecrat movement failed.

## Table 14: American Economic Regions, 1970

| | Total Population (thousands) | Major Metropolitan | Minor Metropolitan (% of total) | Non-metropolitan | Percent of Total U.S. Population |
|---|---|---|---|---|---|
| **I.** Northeast Corridor. | 43,866 | 80.3% | 8.7% | 11.0% | 21.6% |
| **II.** Springfield-Buffalo. | 7,233 | 57.7 | 11.0 | 31.3 | 3.6 |
| **III.** Southeast ........ | 25,164 | 31.8 | 22.2 | 46.0 | 12.4 |
| **IV.** Gulf ............. | 15,734 | 24.1 | 21.8 | 54.1 | 7.7 |
| **V.** Southern Pacific .. | 21,110 | 79.6 | 12.9 | 7.5 | 10.4 |
| **VI.** Northern Pacific .. | 6,774 | 41.9 | 14.8 | 46.3 | 3.3 |
| Subtotal— Rimland .... | 119,881 | 59.1 | 14.3 | 26.6 | 59.0 |
| **VII.** Pittsburgh-Detroit.. | 19,731 | 55.0 | 17.9 | 27.1 | 9.7 |
| **VIII.** Chicago-Milwaukee. | 14,253 | 67.0 | 15.5 | 17.5 | 7.0 |
| **IX.** Border ......... | 20,623 | 45.9 | 14.1 | 40.0 | 10.1 |
| **X.** Northwest ........ | 10,236 | 23.0 | 16.6 | 60.4 | 5.0 |
| **XI.** Central West ..... | 5,134 | 34.8 | 15.3 | 49.9 | 2.5 |
| **XII.** Southwest ....... | 13,347 | 35.9 | 30.0 | 34.1 | 6.6 |
| Subtotal— Heartland .... | 83,324 | 46.5 | 18.2 | 35.3 | 41.0 |
| Total U.S. . | 203,205 | 54.0 | 15.9 | 30.1 | 100.0 |

Note: These regions have been defined by classifying counties rather than states and adding up the totals for every county included in each region. For the different practices of the Bureau of the Census and the Bureau of Economic Analysis, see Appendix A.

Sources: 1970 Census of Population; The Conference Board.

Before delineating these twelve regions, however, it is necessary to present two disclaimers to the reader. First, one must note the difference between ascertaining an important development and measuring its extent. Thus, the evidence that the United States is developing its middle section is very difficult to doubt. Measuring the extent of this middle in 1970, however, is subject to debate at all times because one can never settle

# American Economic Regions, 1970

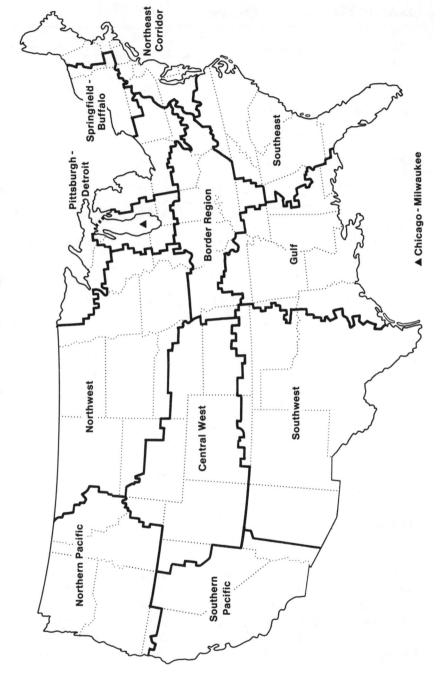

Springfield - Buffalo

Northeast Corridor

Pittsburgh - Detroit

Southeast

Border Region

Gulf

▲ Chicago - Milwaukee

Northwest

Central West

Southwest

Northern Pacific

Southern Pacific

conclusively the problem of just where the middle ends and the extremes begin. There are clear cases where a metropolitan area manifestly belongs in the "heartland" such as Cincinnati. There are other cases, however, where making the right call is very difficult. One may cite Birmingham, Alabama, as such a case. The "heartland" or "border" has been extending itself southward into Kentucky and Tennessee. Has it extended as far as northern Alabama, however? It would be futile to expect conclusive evidence on such points. Therefore, in dealing with this dilemma, it has been decided to err on the side of caution and not depart too far from the old three-way split. As a result, the extent of the "heartland" may be underestimated and the extent of the "rimland" correspondingly overestimated.

Secondly, one must disclaim any attempt in this brief work to delineate the "real" regions of the United States. Social reality has at least three aspects, the legal, the political, and the economic. State lines may be legal fictions but they exert a very real influence on the everyday lives of the residents of each state. Furthermore, political boundaries often diverge from economic boundaries, even though they may mutually influence each other. Thus, an approximation to the "real" regions of the United States would have to be substantially lengthier than the brief sketch of economic regions presented in this work, and two major metropolitan areas might be very different in many other respects even though they may be grouped together for economic reasons. One may cite as an example Houston and New Orleans which have been grouped together in the Gulf region. If one looks only at economic factors, it is clear that these two areas are very much alike. Both are large ports, the centers of far-flung international operations, and their wages are lower than the average for the United States. Yet, as the data on population density presented in the supporting tables shows, the social reality of New Orleans is very different from that of Houston. New Orleans, a much "older" urban area, has a core with a very high density of population while Houston is a new "spread-out" urban area. Consequently, there are weighty reasons for classifying Houston along with Dallas-Ft. Worth in the "heartland" rather than with New Orleans in the "rimland" in addition to the fact that Houston and New Orleans are divided by a state line. Nevertheless, these reasons are not economic, and their consideration has been postponed to subsequent works where each region can be examined in turn. For the moment, certain qualifications that would bring out more detail must be sacrificed for the sake of presenting a picture of the whole that can be followed with relative ease.

# A Survey of the Rimland

America's rimland probably contained 120 million inhabitants, or 59 percent of the population, in 1970. A majority of its population (54 percent) is concentrated in two regions, the Northeast Corridor and the Southern Pacific, which have the greatest proportion in the nation of their populations in major metropolitan areas (80 percent). These two regions, with their heavy concentrations of population in the New York SCA and the Los Angeles SCA, have much in common as far as the structure of their economies is concerned. Of course, they are at opposite ends of the continent and face opposite parts of the world. Until some years ago, the Asia trade was only a hopeful speculation for the Far West, but the development of several Asian nations, particularly Japan, has now made this trade a solid reality. Their high degree of urbanization, their diversified urban economies, their options for trading with other parts of the world, and the great distance between them provide very few incentives for trade between these two regions.

On the other hand, the Southeast (accounting for about 21 percent of the population on the rimland) has a very different structure from the Northeast Corridor: only 32 percent of the population is in major metropolitan areas and most of these are small ones. This signals substantial comparative advantages between the Southeast and the Northeast Corridor, and where comparative advantages exist trade springs up. Thus, one can expect transportation from North to South to continue developing. The Northeast Corridor and the Southern Pacific regions are bound together by the common interests of large metropolitan areas, but the former is bound to the Southeast by the law of comparative advantage. Furthermore, its proximity to the Northeast Corridor gives the Southeast an advantage over the Gulf region, which may explain the more rapid development of manufacturing in the Southeast. The latter is closer to the large market formed by the Northeast Corridor, the largest regional market in the United States. Indeed, it seems that if it were not for the great mineral resources of the Gulf region—which have spurred the growth of Houston and many of its minor metropolitan areas—this region would have experienced much greater emigration than it did between 1950 and 1970, or a lower rate of increase in per capita income. Much the same situation prevails on the West Coast but on a smaller scale, between the Southern Pacific and Northern Pacific regions. The difference is that the region with a large nonmetropolitan population relative to its total population lies to the North. Here again, however, the logic of the law of comparative advantage suggests the growth of trade from South to North rather than from East to West.

Both coasts, although now relatively independent of each other economically, show intense interest in pressing their communications and transportation systems into the interior of the United States. This has resulted in the relative stagnation of the economy of the Mississippi Valley. Trade in the United States, while flowing North-South along its coasts, tends to run East-West from the interior, providing strong links between the "rimland" and the "heartland."

## Northeast Corridor

There are very few regions in the world that can compare with the Northeast Corridor in size and extent of urbanization—perhaps the closest approximation being the lower Rhine Valley. In the United States, the most similar region is the Southern Pacific. The Northeast Corridor contained 44 million inhabitants in 1970 (22 percent of the U.S. population) compared to 21 million in the Southern Pacific (10 percent of the U.S. population). Although both the Northeast Corridor and the Southern Pacific regions had roughly the same proportion of their population in major metropolitan areas in 1970 (80 percent), the Northeast Corridor stretches through thirteen states from Maine to Virginia and is more than double the size of the Southern Pacific region (see Table 14). It contains ten major metropolitan areas and sixteen minor metropolitan areas.[2]

The Northeast Corridor contains three important ports that have always competed strongly with each other for commerce: Boston, New York, and Philadelphia. It has been extended southward by the rapid growth of Washington, D.C., since the 1930's—a result of the expansion of Federal Government employment.

In the competition for commerce, New York has come to overshadow Boston and Philadelphia and to dominate the Northeast Corridor. In 1970, the New York SCA accounted for 50 percent of the population in the ten major metropolitan areas in the Northeast Corridor. Its business district employed 816,000 workers, compared to only 110,000 in Philadelphia and 79,000 in Boston. Manhattan is the center of one of the most complex and intensive transportation networks in the world, which

[2] For a description and definition of the Northeast Corridor, see Jean Gottman, *Megalopolis*. Cambridge, Mass.: The M.I.T. Press, 1964.

stretches into northern New Jersey and southeastern Connecticut. Thus, the Northeast Corridor is characterized by a very large bulge in population and population density at its center, in New York (or, more precisely, Manhattan).

Table 15:   Northeast Corridor—Major Metropolitan Areas in 1970

| | Population (in thousands) | | | | Population Density (inhabitants per square mile) | |
|---|---|---|---|---|---|---|
| | Total | Old Urbanized Area | New Urbanized Area | Outskirts | Old Urbanized Area | New Urbanized Area |
| New York SCA..... | 17,430 | 12,500 | 4,230 | 700 | 9,130 | 3,170 |
| Philadelphia-Wilmington SCA . | 5,190 | 3,020 | 1,370 | 800 | 8,430 | 2,710 |
| Boston SCA ....... | 3,710 | 1,860 | 1,330 | 520 | 5,380 | 2,510 |
| Washington, D.C. ... | 2,860 | 1,240 | 1,240 | 380 | 6,970 | 3,920 |
| Baltimore ......... | 2,070 | 1,110 | 470 | 490 | 7,330 | 2,960 |
| Hartford ......... | 1,040 | 380 | 220 | 440 | 3,810 | 2,030 |
| Providence ....... | 850 | 400 | 400 | 50 | 2,780 | 3,930 |
| New Haven ........ | 740 | 200 | 260 | 280 | 4,250 | 1,390 |
| Worcester, Mass. ... | 640 | 190 | 60 | 390 | 4,280 | 1,480 |
| Allentown-Bethlehem. | 550 | 220 | 150 | 180 | 4,460 | 2,960 |
| Total ...... | 35,080 | 21,120 | 9,730 | 4,230 | 7,562 | 2,928 |
| Percent of Total: | | 60.2% | 27.7% | 12.1% | | |

Source: See Appendix B.

The northern center of the Northeast Corridor is Boston, another focus for an intensive network of transportation that reaches to Providence, R.I., in the south, Worcester, Mass., in the west, and Nashua-Manchester, N.H., a minor metropolitan area, in the north. The Interstate Highway System has reduced the travel time between Worcester, Providence and Boston. For many purposes, many services locating in Boston find that they can also supply Worcester and Providence, and the Bureau of Economic Analysis treats all three major metropolitan areas as one "economic area."

The extension of Boston's roads has led to extensive suburbanization at low population densities around Boston, which has grown around two former satellites, Lowell and Brockton, since 1950. Further suburbanization would engulf the Lawrence-Haverhill urbanized area to the north and extend close to the Nashua-Manchester minor metropolitan area in New Hampshire. Providence and Worcester have also suburbanized extensively; the former is barely separated from Fall River-New Bedford, while the latter now includes a former satellite of Boston, Fitchburg-Leominster. Thus, urban New England today, as an economic unit, consists mainly of three major metropolitan areas—Boston, Worcester and Providence—and three minor metropolitan areas—Nashua-Manchester, Lawrence-Haverhill, and Fall River-New Bedford—all closely integrated by the transportation network that centers in Boston. There are four other centers of population that can be said to be in Boston's hinterland, although connections are more distant. In eastern Connecticut, there is New London-Norwich; in Maine, there are Portland, Lewiston-Auburn, and Bangor. Boston has an extensive hinterland to the north which is very sparsely populated and, in some respects, is well located for serving the Canadian maritime provinces.

South of Boston along the Northeast corridor, two small major metropolitan areas, Hartford and New Haven, probably have more economic affinities with New York than with Boston. Twenty years ago, these two major metropolitan areas might have been treated together as a separate unit from New York, but once again the extension of interstate highways in the postwar period has made them a part of the entire transportation planning area which centers in New York. New Haven has experienced the more extensive suburbanization. In 1950, its urbanized area extended over 47 square miles, but in twenty years it added 191 square miles (part of it, however, due to conurbation with Bridgeport). Since Hartford was also extending its urbanized area substantially, and New York was extending into Fairfield County in Connecticut, there has evolved a very extensive territory of low urban population densities with three high-density centers at Hartford, New Haven, and Bridgeport. This area has a higher proportion of manufacturing than New York. Many New York manufacturers moved their operations here because they were unable to find land at reasonable prices for expansion of their capacity in the New York State part of the New York urbanized area. Much the same process has been at work to the south of New York City in New Jersey and, indeed, the scarcity of land in New York has driven some businesses as far as Pennsylvania.[3]

The Philadelphia-Wilmington SCA is overshadowed by its proximity to New York. Although it is the fourth largest metropolitan area in the

[3] A successful manufacturer finds it hard to remain in New York City, for he has little room to expand his plant. As a consequence, there is a continuous "export" of manufacturing jobs from New York to its surroundings. See Select Committee on the Economy, New York State Assembly, *Industry in New York: A Time of Transition*, New York State Legislative Document No. 12, 1974.

United States, it accounts for only 15 percent of the population in major metropolitan areas in the Northeast Corridor. If it were located in another region, it would be the capital of that region. At present, it forms an important but smaller part of the central portion of the Northeast Corridor. Philadelphia and Wilmington have grown together, but other urbanized areas in the Philadelphia region are separated by rural land from Philadelphia. The most important of these is Allentown-Bethlehem. There are other sizable concentrations of population around Philadelphia, however, which form part of the Northeast Corridor. Three are in New Jersey: Trenton, Atlantic City and Vineland-Millville. Six are in eastern Pennsylvania: Wilkes-Barre, Scranton, Reading, Harrisburg, Lancaster and York. Although, unlike New York City, Philadelphia has not grown into a large number of its satellites, there is a considerable population that surrounds it on all sides. This makes the Philadelphia section of the Northeast Corridor second only to the New York section with respect to the density of population and the intensiveness of the utilization of land.

The newest and southernmost section of the Northeast is the Baltimore-Washington axis. Washington and Baltimore belong together not only because they are close to each other geographically, but because they complement each other. Washington does not have a port or good connections to the West, Baltimore has both. As a result, transportation functions and manufacturing are centered in Baltimore, for a business that settles there can easily ship to Washington and yet maintain its options for shipping to other sections of the nation—or to other parts of the world.

Washington, D.C., has developed not merely as a government town but also as a center for "advanced services." Its business district employed 128,000 in 1970 and was the fourth largest in the nation (following New York, Chicago and San Francisco-San Jose). Washington's growth benefited Baltimore and, at the same time, the closeness of Baltimore furnishes cheap and ready supplies to Washington. Due to this complementarity, transportation facilities between Baltimore and Washington have been intensively developed. This last section of the Northeast corridor has no minor metropolitan areas nor does it have an extensive hinterland. It is bounded by other economic regions: the "heartland" to the west and the Southeast to the south.

At first view, the Northeast Corridor appears to be no more than a heavily utilized trunkline stretching through urbanized territory from Washington to Boston. Certainly, this view is not incorrect insofar as long-distance transportation is concerned. With respect to short hauls, however, there are four relatively independent networks of transportation and communication. The largest and most intensively used is centered in New York; it is followed by the ones centered in Philadelphia, Boston and Washington-Baltimore, respectively. The old urbanized areas at the center of the New York and Philadelphia systems of short-distance transportation have very high population densities, 9,130 inhabitants per square mile for New York and 8,430 for Philadelphia. Baltimore is below this high level at 7,330 inhabitants per square mile. The two centers at the extremities of the Northeast Corridor, Washington and Boston, have substantially reduced the population density of their old urbanized areas.[4]

New York not only has the highest population densities, but it accounts for 59 percent of the entire population residing in areas in the Northeast Corridor urbanized prior to 1950. The reason is that it was one of five major metropolitan areas that succeeded in intensifying the use of its old urbanized area between 1950 and 1970. Some parts declined and others grew. On balance, the old urbanized area increased its density of population slightly. Thus, due mainly to the dominance of New York, newly urbanized areas accounted for only 28 percent of the population of the ten major metropolitan areas in the Northeast Corridor and the outskirts of these urbanized areas for only 12 percent. The entire area has, on the whole, preserved its heritage from the second phase of urbanization, particularly in its central portion.

This fact gives the Northeast Corridor a unique comparative advantage with respect to the rest of the United States (with the possible exception of the Los Angeles area that will be discussed below). It is an ideal location for small establishments relying on "external economies" (for example, shippers that use common carriers rather than their own transportation facilities and equipment). It is also an ideal location for establishments that face great uncertainty and, therefore, must keep their fixed costs to a minimum (for example, the high-fashion lines of women's garments). At the same time, it is at a comparative disadvantage with respect to "greenfield" developments, operations with very high fixed costs, and generally all establishments with routine procedures of purchasing, production and marketing. The Standard Industrial Code shows that the Northeast Corridor has nearly every industry found in metropolitan areas,

---

[4] Washington is not as thickly settled as appears at first sight from the data for population densities. It has hardly any manufacturing, and thus its residential areas have fewer inhabitants per square mile than cities with comparable densities but many square miles urbanized for factories and transportation facilities.

but data for establishments show that a smaller scale of industry prevails in the Northeast Corridor. It pays the Northeast Corridor to concentrate on small, flexible establishments facing great uncertainty and to trade with less-developed parts of the nation for those products and services that can be produced by more standardized and predictable processes.[5]

## Springfield-Buffalo

The Springfield-Buffalo section of the Northeast is considerably simpler in structure than the Northeast Corridor (see Table 16). It is composed mainly of five major metropolitan areas located on the line of transportation between Cleveland and Boston, which roughly parallels the St. Lawrence Seaway. These five major metropolitan areas—Buffalo, Rochester, Albany-Schenectady, Syracuse, and Springfield, Massachusetts— contain 58 percent of the population in this area. Three minor metropolitan areas, Utica-Rome and Binghamton in New York, and Pittsfield, Massachusetts account for 11 percent. Thus, there is a considerable portion of the population (31 percent) residing in nonmetropolitan areas.

What differentiates this section of the Northeast from the Northeast Corridor is not only a different line of transportation, but also an abundance of open space between its metropolitan areas. At the eastern end, Springfield, Pittsfield and Albany-Schenectady form a lightly urbanized zone of considerable extent in area but with a population of only 1.5 million. (Springfield is difficult to classify. It is separated from Worcester by open land but it rests on the fringes of Hartford.) This section rests on the fringes of the Northeast Corridor. To the north of this zone, the land is only lightly settled. As one moves west along the old Erie Canal, one encounters open land to the south as well as the north at Utica-Rome and Syracuse. At the same time, the Canadian frontier draws closer. This small region (4 percent of the U.S. population) is completed by the two lake ports, Rochester on Lake Ontario opposite Toronto and Buffalo on Lake Erie.

No one major metropolitan area dominates this region, although the largest, Buffalo, accounts for about 32 percent of the population in its

---

[5] This does not mean, however, that the Northeast Corridor is not a suitable location for big *enterprises*. One must distinguish between *establishments* and *enterprises* or *businesses*. A big enterprise, for example, can be made up of either one huge establishment (such as an integrated steel mill) or it can be composed of many small establishments (such as a retail chain). The reverse is not true, however, for if an establishment is large, e.g., the Southern Pacific Railroad, then the enterprise has to be large.

**Table 16:  Springfield-Buffalo—Major Metropolitan Areas in 1970**

| | | Population (in thousands) | | | Population Density (inhabitants per square mile) | |
|---|---|---|---|---|---|---|
| | Total | Old Urbanized Area | New Urbanized Area | Outskirts | Old Urbanized Area | New Urbanized Area |
| Buffalo ........... | 1,350 | 610 | 480 | 260 | 6,010 | 4,240 |
| Rochester ......... | 880 | 360 | 240 | 280 | 5,500 | 3,010 |
| Albany-Schenectady.. | 720 | 230 | 250 | 240 | 4,320 | 2,610 |
| Syracuse ......... | 630 | 230 | 140 | 260 | 5,280 | 2,760 |
| Springfield, Mass... | 580 | 350 | 160 | 70 | 2,110 | 2,280 |
| Total ...... | 4,160 | 1,780 | 1,270 | 1,110 | 4,130 | 3,068 |
| Percent of Total | | 42.7% | 30.6% | 26.7% | | |

Source: See Appendix B.

major metropolitan areas. Buffalo is also the major metropolitan area with the highest population densities, despite its concentration on heavy manufacturing. None of the major metropolitan areas in this region, however, are utilizing their old urbanized areas as intensively as they were twenty years ago. Their small size and relative isolation has meant that there has been a very great amount of suburbanization. One finds that only 43 percent of their population resides in the old urbanized areas, 31 percent is in new urbanized areas, and 27 percent in the suburban outskirts. This region does not have the heavy "infrastructure" of the Northeast Corridor. This means a comparative advantage with respect to operations with high fixed costs that allows it to trade profitably with the huge market to its east in the Northeast Corridor.

## Southeast

The crescent of land corresponding to the old Confederacy and stretching from Richmond to Houston could be included as one region within the rimland, but there is a significant difference in orientation between the Southeast and the Gulf regions. The Southeast is, for the most part, oriented toward Europe and its lines of communication run from East to West into the interior of the continent. The Gulf region, by contrast, is centered in New Orleans and the Mississippi and faces the Caribbean and the Panama Canal. Its lines of communication stretch inland towards the north. Peninsular Florida is a distinctive region in its own right. It has as large a proportion of its population in major metropolitan areas as the Northeast Corridor or the Southern Pacific regions, but it contains less than 4 million inhabitants. It has been joined to the Southeast in this analysis because its *transportation lines,* land, air and sea, make the Southeast the logical zone to which it can look for supplies (see Table 17). It is likely that the rapid growth of peninsular Florida has done much to stimulate the growth of the Southeast by furnishing a nearby market for its surplus produce.

**Table 17:  Southeast—Major Metropolitan Areas in 1970**

| | Population (in thousands) | | | Population Density (inhabitants per square mile) | |
|---|---|---|---|---|---|
| Total | Old Urbanized Area | New Urbanized Area | Outskirts | Old Urbanized Area | New Urbanized Area |
| Miami SCA ........ 2,230 | 610 | 1,510 | 110 | 5,300 | 3,070 |
| Atlanta ........... 1,380 | 500 | 670 | 210 | 4,710 | 2,050 |
| Tampa-St. Petersburg 1,010 | 330 | 530 | 150 | 3,000 | 2,950 |
| Norfolk-<br>Newport News SCA 970 | 370 | 560 | 40 | 5,970 | 1,470 |
| Birmingham ....... 740 | 330 | 230 | 180 | 3,320 | 1,810 |
| Greensboro -<br>Winston-Salem ... 610 | 190 | 200 | 220 | 4,040 | 1,520 |
| Jacksonville ...... 530 | 240 | 290 | 0 | 5,000 | 990 |
| Richmond ........ 520 | 240 | 180 | 100 | 5,000 | 1,860 |
| Total ....... 7,990 | 2,810 | 4,170 | 1,010 | 4,731 | 2,057 |
| Percent of Total: | 35.1% | 52.1% | 12.6% | | |

Source: See Appendix B.

If peninsular Florida is joined to the Southeast to form one region, then the nonmetropolitan portion of the population turns out to have been slightly in a minority in 1970, accounting for 46 percent of the total population of this large region. (It contains 12 percent of the total population of the United States). The structure of the metropolitan sector of this region, outside of peninsular Florida, is very different from that of the Northeast. With the exception of Atlanta and its satellites, the metropolitan sector is composed of many relatively independent minor metropolitan areas, plus five small major metropolitan areas: Norfolk-Newport News SCA, Birmingham, Greensboro - Winston-Salem, Jacksonville and Richmond.[6] In addition, there are numerous large towns in the

[6] Since 1970, the Bureau of the Census has redefined two minor metropolitan areas, Charlotte and Greenville, to make them small major metropolitan areas; Charlotte-Gastonia, N.C., and Greenville-Spartanburg, S.C.

nonmetropolitan section of this region that could qualify as minor metropolitan areas if they had central cities with a population of 50,000. There are nineteen such large towns in addition to twenty-five minor metropolitan areas.

The urban sector of this region, outside of peninsular Florida, is singularly diffuse and reflects its past history. It attracted the textile industry due to lower wages in small towns, and wood-processing due to the availability of lumber and pulp. The whole region from Richmond through Jacksonville to Birmingham may be termed an "immature" economy, compared to the "mature" economy of the Northeast Corridor. As such, it tends to attract relatively self-sufficient enterprises producing staples with a fairly predictable demand (e.g., synthetic-fiber mills). It is doubtful, however, that this region will continue to attract low-wage industries, for the wage differential between this region and the rest of the nation has narrowed very rapidly in the postwar period. In fact, some major metropolitan areas outside this region (e.g., Providence, R.I.) have a lower per capita income than some major metropolitan areas in the Southeast (such as Richmond and Atlanta). Of course, the differential persists in the smaller major metropolitan areas as well as in the minor ones. Tampa-St. Petersburg, Norfolk-Newport News SCA, Birmingham and Jacksonville are all below the national average of per capita income, while Greensboro-Winston-Salem is at the national average. Yet, it is doubtful whether the narrowed differential of today is a decisive factor. Thus, the future growth of this region appears to depend on expanding markets plus the ready availability of plant sites with good access to transportation. A chief disadvantage appears to be the labor imbalances that tend to develop more suddenly in minor metropolitan areas and even in the smaller major metropolitan areas.

An indication of the relative newness of the infrastructure of the Southeast is the low proportion of its population in major metropolitan areas that was residing in 1970 in areas urbanized prior to 1950. These old urbanized areas accounted for only 35 percent of the population in major metropolitan areas. In the Miami SCA, the old urbanized area of Miami was being utilized more intensively in 1970 than 1950, an indication that the price of land therein has risen sharply. Nevertheless, growth has been so rapid and suburbanization so extensive that only 27 percent of its population was contained in its old urbanized area in 1970. In the other seven major metropolitan areas in the Southeast, growth has not been as spectacular (with the possible exception of Tampa-St. Petersburg) but it has been above the national average (with the exception of Birmingham).

In addition, all seven, unlike Miami, are using their old urbanized areas less intensively than in 1950. Thus, most of the population in these eight major metropolitan areas is located in new urbanized areas (52 percent) with a minority in the suburban outskirts (13 percent).

## Gulf

Repeated predictions that the Mississippi Valley would form the heart of a mighty empire, dating from before the Louisiana Purchase, have not been borne out. Up until 1896, yellow fever could have been considered a cause, but its elimination makes it evident that the competition of eastern ports has been the chief factor. From Boston to Jacksonville, numerous East Coast port cities have made every possible effort to expand their trade area beyond the Appalachians, and their efforts have been successful. The opening of the St. Lawrence Seaway has further reduced the influence of the Mississippi Valley. It is frequently cheaper to ship from the center of America to Europe via Toledo on Lake Erie and then along the St. Lawrence than to ship south to New Orleans from where the ships have to double back to the North again. Thus, this region, which forms a triangle with its base stretching from Pensacola in Florida to Houston in Texas and a broad apex centered on Memphis, was 54 percent nonmetropolitan in 1970. It has more than its fair share of minor metropolitan areas, 18 in 1970 containing 22 percent of its population. Thus, the proportion of its population in its three major metropolitan areas was very low, 24 percent (compared with the national average of 54 percent).

The Gulf region has an important share of the nation's population

### Table 18:   Gulf—Major Metropolitan Areas in 1970

| | Population (in thousands) | | | | Population Density (inhabitants per square mile) | |
|---|---|---|---|---|---|---|
| | Total | Old Urbanized Area | New Urbanized Area | Outskirts | Old Urbanized Area | New Urbanized Area |
| Houston .......... | 1,980 | 840 | 840 | 300 | 3,113 | 3,123 |
| New Orleans ....... | 1,050 | 630 | 340 | 80 | 6,120 | 4,200 |
| Memphis .......... | 770 | 410 | 250 | 110 | 3,730 | 2,910 |
| Total ....... | 3,800 | 1,880 | 1,430 | 490 | 3,892 | 3,280 |
| Percent of Total: | | 49.5% | 37.6% | 12.9% | | |

Source: See Appendix B.

(about 8 percent or 16 million inhabitants in 1970), but only about 4 million resided in Houston, New Orleans, and Memphis, the three major metropolitan areas in this region. Houston, the largest, accounted for 52 percent of the major metropolitan residents and is the major metropolitan area that has grown most rapidly in this region. It has the most extensive new urbanized areas and outskirts.

New Orleans, on the other hand, had been a trading center since earliest times. Thus, about 60 percent of its residents are contained by the area urbanized prior to 1950, despite the fact that it is being used less intensively than in 1950. These two cities show very diverse population densities: high in New Orleans and low in Houston. Memphis, the smallest of the three, follows the pattern of Houston—low population densities with hardly any difference between population densities in the old and in the new urbanized areas.

## Southern Pacific

The Southern Pacific region is contained nearly entirely by one state, California. The state of Hawaii and two minor metropolitan areas in Nevada (Las Vegas and Reno) account for only a very small proportion of its population. Like the Northeast Corridor, it has 80 percent of its population in major metropolitan areas, and is dominated by one large major metropolitan area, Los Angeles, which accounts for 50 percent of the population in major metropolitan areas in this region.

Los Angeles has not only grown into its former satellites in Orange County, but it is surrounded to the south by San Diego and to the west by Riverside-San Bernardino, two other major metropolitan areas. To its north, there are two rapidly growing minor metropolitan areas, Oxnard-Ventura and Santa Barbara. Thus, the southern section of the Southern Pacific region contains a population of nearly 12 million. This heavy concentration of population has driven up the price of land. Therefore, over the twenty years since 1950, Los Angeles (the original "spread-out" city) has been steadily increasing the density of its population. In 1970, only one-third of its residents were contained by areas urbanized after 1950. Two-thirds were concentrated at a population density of roughly 6,400 per square mile in the area that had been urbanized prior to 1950 at a relatively low population density of 4,600 per square mile. Notable about the Los Angeles SCA is the high population density of its new urbanized areas, 4,000 per square mile, higher than the population density of San Diego's old urbanized area.

All the foregoing points to a scarcity of land in Los Angeles and to a very extensive network of short-haul transportation providing a very large market. Consequently, Los Angeles appears to be approaching the same stage New York was 20 years ago, when it had to rely on the continuous generation of new, small, high-risk establishments to maintain its economy. Its successful enterprises are likely to move to outlying areas once they have become established, routinized their procedures, and want to expand their capacity.

Unlike the Northeast Corridor, the Southern Pacific region does not have a bulge of population and population density at its center, but two bulges—one at the north and one at the south of the region. Fresno is in the center, but the lack of a good port and of connections to the east have inhibited its development in the past. Any business locating in the center of the Southern Pacific region acquires the option of shipping either to the Los Angeles SCA or to the San Francisco-San Jose SCA, but loses the options of either shipping east or to the ever more important

**Table 19: Southern Pacific—Major Metropolitan Areas in 1970**

| | | Population (in thousands) | | | Population Density (inhabitants per square mile) | |
| --- | --- | --- | --- | --- | --- | --- |
| | Total | Old Urbanized Area | New Urbanized Area | Outskirts | Old Urbanized Area | New Urbanized Area |
| Los Angeles SCA.... | 8,450 | 5,550 | 2,800 | 100 | 6,370 | 3,990 |
| San Francisco-San Jose SCA.... | 4,430 | 2,020 | 2,000 | 410 | 5,000 | 3,270 |
| San Diego ........ | 1,360 | 480 | 720 | 160 | 3,610 | 3,140 |
| Riverside-San Bernardino .. | 1,150 | 150 | 440 | 560 | 2,460 | 1,770 |
| Sacramento ....... | 800 | 200 | 430 | 170 | 4,760 | 2,130 |
| Honolulu ......... | 630 | 290 | 150 | 190 | 3,410 | 5,000 |
| Total ....... | 16,820 | 8,690 | 6,540 | 1,590 | 5,643 | 3,206 |
| Percent of Total: | | 51.7% | 38.9% | 9.5% | | |

Source: See Appendix B.

Asian markets. This structure reflects to some extent the former "colonial" status of California's economy relative to the manufacturing belt, when San Francisco and Los Angeles relied on processing and shipping agricultural and mineral produce to large cities in the North in return for their manufactures. Today, however, the center of the California economy is showing rapid growth, perhaps because the market has grown so large that many more enterprises are willing to take the chance of being limited by its size.

The northern bulge is centered on the San Francisco-San Jose SCA. This sector has one district, San Francisco-Oakland, that was developed— substantially before Los Angeles—along the lines of Northern cities. Consequently, it had high population densities in 1950, especially in San Francisco. Unlike Los Angeles, however, in the postwar period it has reduced somewhat the population density of its old urbanized areas and suburbanized so extensively that it has been joined to its former satellite, San Jose, which was showing even more rapid growth on the basis of a sharp increase in manufacturing. The San Francisco-San Jose SCA now has a population of 4.4 million. On the west, it is circled by one major metropolitan area, Sacramento, and two minor metropolitan areas, Stockton and Modesto. To the north, there is Santa Rosa and, to the south, Salinas-Monterey, two more minor metropolitan areas. Thus, San Francisco-San Jose and its "zone of influence" constitute a concentration of population of about 6 million, that is, about one-half the population of Los Angeles and its "zone of influence."[7] As far as can be inferred from population densities, land in this northern bulge of the Southern Pacific region is not cheap, but it has not attained the high scarcity value that it has in Los Angeles. After many years of lagging behind the spectacular growth of Los Angeles and its surroundings, this region in the north appears at present to be growing more rapidly. It appears to have the advantage of a substantial infrastructure in the old San Francisco-Oakland area, which can nourish small establishments in the center, without the very high prices of land that would discourage "greenfield" developments on its outskirts, particularly around San Jose.

## Northern Pacific

The Northern Pacific region has great natural resources: farms, forests and mines. It also has cheap energy in the form of hydroelectric power from the Columbia River watershed. Thus, 46 percent of its population resides in nonmetropolitan areas compared with only 8 percent in the Southern Pacific. It is very great in area but sparsely populated, so that it accounts for only 3 percent of the population of the United States. Thus, it is very similar to the Central West (discussed in the following

[7] These "zones of influence" are outlined in Walton A. Bean, *California, An Interpretive History*. New York: McGraw-Hill Book Co., 1968.

**Table 20: Northern Pacific—Major Metropolitan Areas in 1970**

|  | Population (in thousands) | | | | Population Density (inhabitants per square mile) | |
|  | Total | Old Urbanized Area | New Urbanized Area | Outskirts | Old Urbanized Area | New Urbanized Area |
|---|---|---|---|---|---|---|
| Seattle-Tacoma SCA. | 1,830 | 760 | 810 | 260 | 4,100 | 2,270 |
| Portland, Oregon ... | 1,010 | 500 | 330 | 180 | 4,390 | 2,160 |
| Total ....... | 2,840 | 1,260 | 1,140 | 440 | 4,210 | 2,235 |
| Percent of Total: | | 44.3% | 40.2% | 15.5% | | |

Source: See Appendix B.

chapter), particularly since its metropolitan population is concentrated in two major metropolitan areas, Seattle-Tacoma SCA and Portland (with its two satellites, Eugene and Salem). Both major metropolitan areas, however, are important ports that look to Asia and to the Southern Pacific region for the closest markets for the produce of farm, forest and mine. On the basis of cheap supplies of electricity, the Seattle-Tacoma SCA has developed an important manufacturing sector, but Portland has remained chiefly a transportation center and processor of raw products. There are only two relatively independent minor metropolitan areas in this region, Spokane in Washington and Boise in Idaho. Nearly all its population is found either in Portland and Seattle-Tacoma or else in relatively small towns that are bases for exploiting the natural resources of the region.[8]

[8] A case can be made up for treating Utah, Idaho, Western Montana, Washington, Oregon, and Alaska along with California as one region named the "Pacific Slope." Yet, life in the metropolitan areas of California has become very distinct from the rest of the Pacific Slope in the last 30 to 40 years. The California economy no longer functions on a heavy base of transportation and natural resources but has come to resemble the Northeast Corridor. For information on the Pacific Slope as a whole, see Earl Pomeroy, *The Pacific Slope, A History*. New York: Alfred A. Knopf, 1968.

# 5.
# The American Heartland

THERE ARE TWO TYPES of "heartland." In many cases, the "heartland" contains the largest city in the nation, sometimes the nation's capital, and dominates the rest of the nation. This is what occurs in such highly centralized nations as France and Great Britain. In the United States, however, there has never been one dominant center, and its largest urban center has always been located in the "rimland." New York's position from 1890 to 1950 is the closest the United States came to having one dominant center, but, although New York may be said to have overshadowed nearly all other urban centers during this period, the urban sector accounted for only 19 percent of the population in 1890 and 58 percent in 1950. Thus, during this period when urban and agricultural forces were competing with each other, New York cannot be said to have dominated the nation, even though it may have set the pace for the urban sector while this sector was rising to account for the majority of the population.

What held for the past, is even more true at present. The two largest urban areas in the United States are in the "rimland," not the "heartland." The United States "heartland" cannot be said to dominate the United States economy. In fact, its estimated population of 83 million is less than the estimated 120 million in the "rimland." Thus, it is apparent that the United States economy is decentralized, despite the unparalleled development of transportation and communications that has been under way since the end of the Civil War.

Of course, the "heartland" has a center, Chicago, but this center accounts for only nine percent of the total population of the "heartland." Consequently, the "heartland" itself is not centralized. This makes description and identification of the "heartland" difficult, just as it is difficult to describe the geographic configuration of the United States economy given the fact that there is no clear hierarchical order by which to classify its urban centers clearly.

In examining the "heartland," one must beware of carrying a certain characteristic of the "heartland" too far, namely, its resistance to foreign customs and foreign ideas. The fact that the "heartland" is likely to represent most firmly the traditions of any nation is true and stems from commonsense observation. But one must beware of generalizing too far from what is merely a tendency to which there are many exceptions. It is more accurate to think of the "heartland" as an area where there is a strong repugnance to faction because it has a vested interest in the unity of the nation in which it is located. It is, in short, like any sort of middle.

## A Survey of the Heartland

It may be estimated that, in 1970, the "heartland" contained about 41 percent of the population of the United States. As indicated in the preceding chapter, this is a conservative estimate. It is a region that tends to trade East-West rather than North-South. However, the East Coast and the West Coast cannot be said to have been inactive in the task of cementing themselves to the heartland. Their ports have actively sought to extend their connections into the center of the United States so that they could develop their own economies on the basis of trading for products that require a large input of natural resources, either as material or as fuel. Free trade and an abundance of raw materials overseas may have loosened these ties (as in the case of the construction of steel mills in the Philadelphia and Baltimore areas in order to take advantage of abundant foreign iron ore), but, if it has now become more difficult for the United States to procure fuel and raw materials abroad, these ties will be strengthened. A return to protectionism would induce the rimland to look for the comparative advantages that give rise to trade at home rather than abroad.

Since 1950, the American heartland has increased its size more through the rapid breakdown of old barriers than through migration to this region. Although there has been migration to the heartland from the South, migration in the United States after World War II has, on balance, favored the seaboard as witnessed by the unparalleled growth of Florida and California. The American "heartland" can be divided into two parts, each with three regions. On the east, there is the area that was settled mainly prior to the Civil War. It is composed of the Pittsburgh-Detroit, Chicago-Milwaukee, and the Border regions. This "old west" contained 55 million inhabitants in 1970, or about two-thirds of the population of the "heartland." It is not as highly urbanized as the Northeast Corridor or the Southern Pacific regions. Yet, in 1970 about 55 percent of its population resided in major metropolitan areas.

On the west, there is the "new west," settled largely after the Civil War. It also has three regions, the Northwest, the Central West, and the Southwest. The new west had 29 million inhabitants in 1970 and only 31 percent of its population is contained in major metropolitan areas. Such low urbanization is matched only by the Southeast and Gulf regions, that is, the old South.

Although it may make sense to count the old and the new wests together at present, there remain sizable differences between these two sections of the "heartland" due to past history, different climates, and different natural resources. Consequently, there are important comparative advantages within the "heartland" itself, and they tie the "heartland" together. For example, a factory in Cleveland is likely to produce the machine tools that are used in Omaha to produce irrigation equipment for farmers further west. The "heartland" is a complex region that is difficult to describe. The "heartland's" regions range from the Chicago-Milwaukee region, where 67 percent of the population resides in major metropolitan areas, to the Northwest, where only 23 percent of the population lives in major metropolitan areas. The diversity is not as great as in the case of the "rimland"—but it is still substantial.

## Pittsburgh-Detroit

This region is a large arc between the coal fields of the Appalachians and the iron mines of the Mesabi Range to the west of Lake Superior. It is dominated by three large major metropolitan areas, Detroit, Cleveland-Akron SCA, and Pittsburgh (see Table 21). Almost one-half of the total population of this region was concentrated in these three centers. There are two other smaller major metropolitan areas, Toledo between Cleveland and Detroit, and Youngstown between Pittsburgh and Cleveland. Fifteen minor metropolitan areas accounted for the remainder of the metropolitan population. Nearly all of these were satellites of either Detroit, Cleveland-Akron SCA, or Pittsburgh. Thus, only 23 percent of the population of this region resided in nonmetropolitan areas. Due to the enterprise of eastern ports, the Pittsburgh-Detroit region has strong links with the Northeast Corridor. Philadelphia has built its transportation and communications facilities with Pittsburgh since the beginning of the 19th century. New York, through the Erie Canal and the New York Central Railroad, achieved even greater success in linking up with Cleveland and other ports on the Great Lakes. Boston was also active in establishing connections.

Despite eastern links, the Pittsburgh-Detroit region has special features that single it out. The St. Lawrence Seaway has given it an all-water route from Lake Erie to Europe and other parts of the world. Yet, it has many options for shipping west, either to the Chicago-Milwaukee or the

Border regions, which together form a market that is almost three-quarters as large as the Northeast. But its principal distinction from the Northeast is probably its proximity to plentiful fuel in the form of coal. This consideration influences manufacturing more than other economic activities that use less fuel, and some industries such as steel much more than others.

**Table 21: Pittsburgh-Detroit—Major Metropolitan Areas in 1970**

| | Population (in thousands) | | | | Population Density (inhabitants per square mile) | |
|---|---|---|---|---|---|---|
| | Total | Old Urbanized Area | New Urbanized Area | Outskirts | Old Urbanized Area | New Urbanized Area |
| Detroit | 4,200 | 2,200 | 1,770 | 230 | 5,560 | 3,720 |
| Cleveland-Akron  SCA | 3,000 | 1,420 | 1,280 | 300 | 3,570 | 2,290 |
| Pittsburgh | 2,400 | 1,160 | 690 | 550 | 4,550 | 2,010 |
| Toledo | 690 | 330 | 160 | 200 | 4,700 | 1,650 |
| Youngstown | 530 | 240 | 150 | 140 | 3,060 | 3,080 |
| Total | 10,820 | 5,350 | 4,050 | 1,420 | 4,473 | 2,659 |
| Percent of Total: | | 49.4% | 37.4% | 13.2% | | |

Source: See Appendix B.

The entire region, therefore, forms a heavily utilized, long-distance trunkline with the centers for short-haul transportation at Pittsburgh, Cleveland and Detroit. Manufacturing accounts for a higher than average proportion of employment in nearly all its metropolitan areas, whether major or minor. In addition, there is a flow of steel from Pittsburgh to metal fabricators along this axis to Detroit and its satellites, so that the region as a whole has a strong comparative advantage in "heavy" industry, whereas the Northeast Corridor excels with respect to "light" industry. This differential promotes trade between the two regions without affecting the vertical integration of manufacturing that is characteristic of this region.

Detroit, on the north, tends to dominate the major metropolitan sector of this region, accounting for 39 percent of the total population in major metropolitan areas. It has grown very rapidly with the automobile age.[1] The Cleveland-Akron SCA has shown less growth than Detroit but more than Pittsburgh.

Pittsburgh is the largest metropolitan area in the nation that has experi-

[1] Since the 1970 Census, one of Detroit's satellites, Flint, has passed the 500,000 population mark and become an additional major metropolitan area in this region.

enced net outmigration during the twenty years from 1950 to 1970. Its growth has been due entirely to the natural increase of its population. The past history of Pittsburgh, its housing market, and its labor market present considerable interest as a precedent for what is likely to occur in Northern major metropolitan areas (see Chapter 3). One thing that is evident is that the net outflow of migrants did not hinder extensive suburb-anization in Pittsburgh. Between 1950 and 1970, Pittsburgh added 342 square miles of newly urbanized areas to the 254 square miles it had in 1950. The population density of its old urbanized area dropped from around 6,000 inhabitants per square mile to around 4,500. Its newly urbanized areas have been developed at a very low population density (for the North) of 2,000 inhabitants per square mile.

Net outmigration may reflect a loss of job opportunities, which produces initial difficulties. But the outmigration relieves some of these difficulties (except for local governments and local businesses which are tied to the area) and presents an opportunity to upgrade the stock of housing and use it less intensively.

The question that remains is whether the "infra-structure"—e.g., sewers, mass transportation facilities, public buildings such as hospitals and schools —can be maintained by a smaller population. The answer depends partly on whether the new suburbanized areas can be induced to use the old urbanized areas for some purposes, and partly on rising incomes that increase the demand for urbanized land. Whatever the answer may be, the experience of Pittsburgh appears to indicate that the departure of young men and women looking for better job opportunities in other metropolitan areas is a better solution than the lowering of wages, particularly if the process is slow and continues over many years. Some highly specialized facilities will inevitably have to be written off completely, but others can be rehabilitated and modernized for new uses.

Currently, both Detroit and the Cleveland-Akron SCA—as well as Pittsburgh—are experiencing a substantial amount of emigration. Major metropolitan areas in this region contain nearly 50 percent of their popu-lation in old urbanized areas. Although this is a lesser proportion than in the Northeast Corridor, it still represents an important heritage from the second phase of U.S. urbanization that cannot be lightly abandoned.

## Chicago-Milwaukee

The Chicago-Milwaukee region hugs the western tip of Lake Michigan and extends its influence into western Michigan. Sixty-seven percent of its population resides in major metropolitan areas, placing it third highest after the Northeast Corridor and the Southern Pacific regions with respect to the proportion of its population residing in major metropolitan areas. Its population of 14 million in 1970, however, is substantially below the population of the Northeast Corridor (44 million) or even of the Southern Pacific (21 million).

This region resembles the adjacent Pittsburgh-Detroit region with respect to its access to iron and coal, the latter being plentiful in southern Illinois. Its chief advantage over other regions is its strategic location for any manufacturer who proposes to ship to all United States and Canadian markets. Chicago is located very close to the center of population of the United States and Canada.

Table 22:   Chicago-Milwaukee—Major Metropolitan Areas in 1970

| | | Population (in thousands) | | | Population Density (inhabitants per square mile) | |
|---|---|---|---|---|---|---|
| | Total | Old Urbanized Area | New Urbanized Area | Outskirts | Old Urbanized Area | New Urbanized Area |
| Chicago .......... | 7,620 | 4,280 | 2,910 | 430 | 6,600 | 3,690 |
| Milwaukee ........ | 1,400 | 760 | 490 | 150 | 7,430 | 1,400 |
| Grand Rapids ...... | 540 | 200 | 150 | 190 | 4,310 | 1,520 |
| Total ....... | 9,560 | 5,240 | 3,550 | 770 | 6,658 | 2,849 |
| Percent of Total: | | 54.8% | 37.1% | 8.1% | | |

Source: See Appendix B.

The entire region, with two horns reaching into western Michigan and eastern Wisconsin, is dominated by the Chicago SCA, which accounts for 53 percent of its total population and 80 percent of its population residing in major metropolitan areas (see Table 22). There are only two other major metropolitan areas, Milwaukee on the northwest horn and Grand Rapids on the northeast horn, but there are ten minor metropolitan areas. The western shore of Lake Michigan is the most highly developed, with two minor metropolitan areas, Racine and Kenosha, between Milwaukee and Chicago. Consequently, this part of Lake Michigan's shore has been nearly entirely urbanized. On the shore between the Indiana portion of the Chicago SCA (Gary-Hammond-East Chicago) and Grand Rapids, however, there are considerable stretches of undeveloped coastline, and these offer considerable opportunities for "greenfield" developments. There is not as much of a shortage of space in the Chicago area as in Los Angeles and New York.

Due to its favorable location with respect to national markets, Chicago exhibited spectacular growth during the second phase of urbanization (1880 to 1950) when national manufactures led the growth of the urban economy. Milwaukee also experienced its principal boom during this period. Consequently, both metropolitan areas entered the postwar period with large, densely populated urbanized areas. In 1950 Chicago had a population density of roughly 7,700 inhabitants per square mile, and Milwaukee one of 8,200. Both have reduced the population densities of their old urbanized areas to 6,600 to 7,400, respectively, and they have developed extensive suburban areas. Chicago now has roughly the same density of population as Los Angeles; the population density of Milwaukee is sharply below that of Los Angeles.

Milwaukee exhibits an exceptional contrast between the population densities of its old and new urbanized areas. Its new urbanized areas have been developed at the very low population density of 1,400 inhabitants per square mile, compared with 3,690 inhabitants per square mile for Chicago. This is an indication of the much greater abundance of open land that is generally to be found in the smaller metropolitan areas. However, because of the great importance of the second phase of urbanization in the development of this region, a larger proportion of the population than in most other regions of the nation, 55 percent, lives in the old urbanized areas. Grand Rapids is the exception because its past growth has been steadier. Its newly urbanized areas and its outskirts account for 63 percent of its population.[2]

## Border Region

The reemergence of the Border region some 100 years after the Civil War is perhaps the most fundamental change in the economic and political geography of the United States (see Table 23). Missouri calls itself the "crossroads" state, but this description fits the entire region, which stretches from the center of West Virginia to the Kansas-Missouri border.[3] There are two main points where roads cross in this region. On the east, Cincinnati, the second largest metropolitan area in the Border region, is

[2] Historically, western Michigan has looked to Chicago, although the state of Michigan has promoted the development of transportation facilities from Detroit to the rest of the state. See F. Clever Bald, *Michigan in Four Centuries*. New York: Harper & Row, 1961.
[3] See Edwin C. McReynolds, *Missouri, A History of the Crossroads State*. Norman, Okla.: University of Oklahoma Press, 1962.

not only closely connected with the entire "old west," but it has important connections with the Northeast Corridor at Baltimore and with the Southeast at Norfolk-Newport News and Atlanta. It forms the apex of a triangle of which the base stretches from Columbus, Ohio, to Indianapolis (along the old National Pike) and which contains three other major metropolitan areas: Columbus, Indianapolis and Dayton, and four minor metropolitan areas—all with substantial manufacturing employment.

On the west, the second crossroad is located at St. Louis. The center of *population* of the United States in 1970 was located just a few miles east of St. Louis. There are many ties between St. Louis and Kansas City, Missouri, on its west, which is the metropolitan area nearest to the *geographical* center of the United States. Thus, St. Louis and Kansas City, along with three minor metropolitan areas, form an "urban corridor," that is, another agglomeration of the population residing in major metropolitan areas in the Border region. The agglomeration north of Cincinnati accounts for 4.5 million inhabitants, and the combination of St. Louis and Kansas City for 3.6 million.

Table 23:  Border Region—Major Metropolitan Areas in 1970

|  | Population (in thousands) | | | | Population Density (inhabitants per square mile) | |
|---|---|---|---|---|---|---|
|  | Total | Old Urbanized Area | New Urbanized Area | Outskirts | Old Urbanized Area | New Urbanized Area |
| St. Louis | 2,360 | 1,010 | 870 | 480 | 4,440 | 3,910 |
| Cincinnati SCA | 1,610 | 700 | 500 | 410 | 4,810 | 2,640 |
| Kansas City, Missouri | 1,250 | 600 | 500 | 150 | 4,010 | 1,460 |
| Indianapolis | 1,110 | 480 | 340 | 290 | 5,800 | 2,170 |
| Columbus, Ohio | 920 | 380 | 380 | 160 | 5,850 | 2,430 |
| Dayton | 850 | 290 | 400 | 160 | 4,600 | 2,480 |
| Louisville | 830 | 430 | 310 | 90 | 6,440 | 2,150 |
| Nashville | 540 | 210 | 240 | 90 | 3,890 | 820 |
| Total | 9,470 | 4,100 | 3,540 | 1,830 | 4,750 | 1,946 |
| Percent of Total: | | 43.3% | 37.4% | 19.3% | | |

Source: See Appendix B.

There are two major metropolitan areas in this region which are relatively unassociated with other major metropolitan areas, Louisville and Nashville. Their combined population amounts to 1.4 million, that is, about 14 percent of the total major metropolitan inhabitants of the Border region.

Thus, there is no single dominating center in the Border region, but rather two centers at its eastern and western ends, Cincinnati and St. Louis. The region is more urban outside of Kentucky, Tennessee and West Virginia, reflecting past trends of economic development, but the sharp difference in income and industries that was formerly evident once one crossed the Ohio River has been narrowed sharply. Thus, the urbanization of the population of the Border region at present is not very far from the United States average. In 1970, 46 percent of its population resided in major metropolitan areas compared with the national average of 54 percent; 14 percent in minor metropolitan areas compared with 16 percent nationally; and 40 percent in nonmetropolitan areas, compared with 30 percent for the whole United States. Consequently, this region is balanced between extremes not only by its geographical position but also in terms of the diversity of its economic and political interests. In fact, its metropolitan population was contained mainly in medium-sized major metropolitan areas.

The relatively large distances among its major metropolitan areas and their moderate size meant that in 1950, when automobile transportation began rapidly to replace mass transportation, the major metropolitan areas in this region had plenty of room to expand. As a result, there has been very extensive suburbanization at low population densities throughout the region, even though the growth of population of these major metropolitan areas has not been high. Thus, suburban population densities average 2,000 inhabitants per square mile. St. Louis appears to be an exception, but actually its high suburban population density is due to the development of a new center, West Port, outside of its old center in St. Louis City. As a result of extensive suburbanization, the population residing in old urbanized areas contained by major metropolitan areas amounted to only 43 percent of the total population in major metropolitan areas; 37 percent was in newly urbanized areas and 20 percent in the outskirts of urbanized areas.

The Border region forms a bridge not only between North and South but also between the old and the new west. The Pittsburgh-Detroit and Chicago-Milwaukee regions are not as heavily major metropolitan as the Northeast or the Southern Pacific regions, but they do contain four very great concentrations of population—the Chicago SCA and Detroit in particular. In none of the regions of the new west does the population in major metropolitan areas form a majority of the population, and, in one region, the Northwest, the nonmetropolitan population is in the majority. The Border region contains an important zone of distribution for the new west, namely, the trade corridor between St. Louis and Kansas City. Outside of this corridor, this region approaches the distribution of population of the new west without, however, departing too far from that of the other two regions of the old west. It has natural resources that can support a nonurban population as well as important urban centers.[4]

## Northwest

In the western portions of the Northwest, the settler had to cope with a scarcity of water and also with long, hard winters. In the eastern portion (that is, in Wisconsin, Iowa, eastern Nebraska, and the southern parts of Minnesota), drought is a lesser danger even though the winters are equally long.[5] Therefore, the value per acre of farm products is much higher.

Table 24: Northwest—Major Metropolitan Areas in 1970

| | | Population (in thousands) | | | Population Density (inhabitants per square mile) | |
|---|---|---|---|---|---|---|
| | Total | Old Urbanized Area | New Urbanized Area | Outskirts | Old Urbanized Area | New Urbanized Area |
| Minneapolis-St. Paul ........ | 1,810 | 880 | 820 | 110 | 3,820 | 1,670 |
| Omaha ............ | 540 | 310 | 180 | 50 | 4,850 | 2,120 |
| Total ....... | 2,350 | 1,190 | 1,000 | 160 | 4,007 | 1,739 |
| Percent of Total: | | 50.6% | 42.6% | 6.8% | | |

Source: See Appendix B.

The entire region has 60 percent of its population residing in nonmetropolitan areas, which is the highest proportion in the nation. It accounts for 5 percent of the population of the United States, contains two major and eleven minor metropolitan areas (see Table 24). The major metropolitan areas, Minneapolis-St. Paul and Omaha (the latter frequently

[4] One must note, of course, that in Ohio, Indiana and Illinois, there has always been a division between "upstate" and "downstate." The "downstate" portions have always had ties with the South. See Walter Havighurst, *The Heartland: Ohio, Indiana, Illinois.* New York: Harper & Row, 1962. See also Irving Leibowitz, *My Indiana.* Englewood Cliffs, N.J.: Prentice-Hall, Inc., 1964.

[5] For a description of some of the western portion of this area, see K. Ross Toole, *Twentieth-Century Montana, A State of Extremes.* Norman, Okla.: University of Oklahoma Press, 1972. For the eastern portion, see Robert C. Nesbitt, *Wisconsin, A History.* Madison, Wis.: University of Wisconsin Press, 1973.

included in the Central West), accounted for 23 percent of the population of this region in 1970. Omaha and Minneapolis-St. Paul differ substantially in size, however, since the latter contains 1.8 million inhabitants and the the former only 0.5 million.

Part of the disparity may be explained by the fact that Minneapolis-St. Paul is the transportation center for a much larger region which extends as far north as the Canadian prairie provinces. Omaha, on the other hand, is sandwiched between Minneapolis-St. Paul on the north and Kansas City on the south. Nevertheless, Minneapolis-St. Paul has developed an important and diversified manufacturing sector. Omaha's manufactures, by contrast, like those of the minor metropolitan areas in Iowa and its border with Illinois (Davenport-Rock Island, Des Moines, Cedar Rapids, Dubuque and Waterloo), are oriented either toward the processing of agricultural products or the fabrication of agricultural implements. The other six minor metropolitan areas in this region are trade centers for nonmetropolitan population. They stretch from Sioux City, on the border of Iowa and Nebraska, to Billings, Montana.

## Central West

In terms of population, the Central West is very small, accounting for only 2.5 percent of the population of the United States (see Table 25). Yet, it covers a vast expanse of territory, part on the plains of Nebraska, Wyoming, Kansas and Colorado and part on the mountains of Wyoming, Idaho, Utah and Colorado. Its two major metropolitan areas, Denver and Salt Lake City, contain a larger proportion of the population than the Northwest, 35 percent rather than 23 percent, but slightly less than the

**Table 25: Central West—Major Metropolitan Areas in 1970**

| | | Population (in thousands) | | | Population Density (inhabitants per square mile) | |
|---|---|---|---|---|---|---|
| | Total | Old Urbanized Area | New Urbanized Area | Outskirts | Old Urbanized Area | New Urbanized Area |
| Denver .............. | 1,230 | 550 | 500 | 180 | 5,240 | 2,480 |
| Salt Lake City...... | 560 | 200 | 280 | 80 | 2,630 | 2,590 |
| Total ....... | 1,790 | 750 | 780 | 260 | 4,144 | 2,516 |
| Percent of Total: | | 41.9% | 43.5% | 14.6% | | |

Source: See Appendix B.

proportion in the Southwest, 36 percent. Proportionally, it has fewer minor metropolitan areas than the Southwest. It has Ogden and Provo-Orem north and south of Salt Lake City, Colorado Springs and Pueblo south of Denver, and Lincoln, the capital of Nebraska, within its borders. Only 15 percent of its population resides in minor metropolitan areas, while 50 percent is located in nonmetropolitan areas. The Central West is very similar to much of the Northwest, being differentiated largely by the fact that it contains a great deal of mountainous territory west of Denver.

Denver is substantially larger than Salt Lake City, but the disparity is not as great as in the case of Minneapolis-St. Paul and Omaha.[6] The region as a whole has benefited from scientific and large-scale management of water resources and from federal highways. Both these factors have enabled it to overcome its two principal handicaps, the scarcity of water and the consequent sparseness of population. Thus, it has shown considerable growth over the postwar period. Nevertheless, it remains the smallest region in terms of population of the United States. Its neighbor to the north, the Northern Pacific, is the second smallest. There is no lack of space in the Central West and consequently population densities are low in its urbanized areas. This makes it very different from the Southern Pacific region to its west.

## Southwest

The Southwest is the most urban part of the "new west." In 1970, it had four major metropolitan areas, the Dallas-Ft. Worth SCA, Phoenix, San Antonio, and Oklahoma City (see Table 26).[7] What is unique about the Southwest is the very high proportion of its population residing in its twenty minor metropolitan areas—30 percent, the highest of any region in the nation. Thus, it is the only part of the new west where the nonmetropolitan population is in a decided minority. The region has a complex structure because it contains two axes of tranportation. One stretches from Kansas City in a southwesterly direction to Houston; the other runs west from Houston to Los Angeles.

There are added complexities because of its boundary with Mexico. In

---

[6] After the 1970 Census, the definition of the Salt Lake City Standard Metropolitan Statistical Area has been changed by including Ogden. This changed definition would give the Salt Lake City area a population of 680,000 in 1970.

[7] But since 1970, two large minor metropolitan areas—Tulsa and El Paso—have passed the 500,000 mark and become major metropolitan areas. Thus, the region at present has six major metropolitan areas.

**Table 26: Southwest—Major Metropolitan Areas in 1970**

| | | Population (in thousands) | | | Population Density (inhabitants per square mile) | |
|---|---|---|---|---|---|---|
| | Total | Old Urbanized Area | New Urbanized Area | Outskirts | Old Urbanized Area | New Urbanized Area |
| Dallas-Ft. Worth SCA | 2,320 | 940 | 1,080 | 300 | 3,590 | 1,330 |
| Phoenix ........... | 970 | 220 | 650 | 100 | 4,000 | 1,950 |
| San Antonio ....... | 860 | 370 | 400 | 90 | 4,120 | 3,020 |
| Oklahoma City ..... | 640 | 230 | 350 | 60 | 3,360 | 1,300 |
| Total ....... | 4,790 | 1,760 | 2,480 | 550 | 3,713 | 1,603 |
| Percent of Total: | | 36.7% | 51.8% | 11.5% | | |

Source: See Appendix B.

the Northwest, there is little difference between the life led in the Canadian and the U.S. prairie provinces. The Southwest portion of the United States, however, borders directly on Latin America, where both language and traditions are very different from those in the United States.

The Southwest has one very large major metropolitan area, the Dallas-Ft. Worth SCA, which accounts for 48 percent of the population residing in major metropolitan areas. In 1970, the Dallas-Ft. Worth SCA contained 2.3 million inhabitants. In 1973, it was the twelfth highest metropolitan area in the nation in terms of total personal income.[8] It has grown rapidly in the postwar period, developing an important manufacturing sector.

It has not, however, grown as rapidly as Phoenix, which could be described as the Miami of the Southwest. Phoenix now has nearly one million inhabitants and is continuing to grow at about 5 percent yearly, while the Dallas-Ft. Worth rate of growth has decelerated considerably. In fact, the Dallas-Ft. Worth SCA experienced some net outmigration in 1970-1973 (see Table 10 in Chapter 3). Its growth came entirely from natural increase, that is, the difference between births and deaths.

San Antonio is nearly as large as Phoenix and has a high growth rate, although not as high as that of Phoenix. Its per capita income is 86 percent of the national average, making it the major metropolitan area that has the lowest wages in the nation. Consequently, it tends to attract low-wage industries. Much the same phenomenon prevails in the minor metropolitan areas on the Mexican border (Brownsville-Harlingen,

[8] See Juan de Torres, "The New Reality of Major U.S. Metro-Areas." *The Conference Board Record,* June, 1975, pp. 54-61.

McAllen-Edinburg, and El Paso). Oklahoma City was in 1970 the fourth and smallest major metropolitan area in this region, being located between Kansas City and the Dallas-Ft. Worth SCA. It has also experienced rapid growth in the postwar period.

The urbanization of the Southwest has occurred largely in the period after World War II and has been very rapid. At the same time, its metropolitan areas are widely separated from each other. They had ample land on which to develop. Thus, population densities in its urbanized areas are the lowest in the nation. They are low not only in the new urbanized areas but also in the old urbanized areas. At the same time, this is the region which, next to the Southeast, has the smallest proportion of the population residing in major metropolitan areas contained within the boundaries of its old urbanized areas. The old urbanized areas of the Southeast contained 35 percent of its major metropolitan population while those in the Southwest contain 37 percent.

The urban environment in this region and in the Southeast are almost opposite to that which exists in the Northeast Corridor and Southern Pacific in terms of the availability of land. The only exception appears to be San Antonio, which is less spread out in both its old and new urbanized areas. This, however, can be explained by its low per capita income, that is, a lower ability to develop and purchase improved land, rather than to any scarcity of land.

# Appendix A:
# Definitions of Regions

     The delineation of the twelve economic regions has drawn on the work of Donald J. Bogue as it has been updated and presented in the 1970 Census of Population. The Bureau of the Census presents 118 economic regions which are divided into many State Economic Areas. It does not attempt to consolidate them into larger regions. The other source used for the purpose of delineating economic regions is the Regional Economic Analysis Division of the Bureau of Economic Analysis. In its October 31, 1974 publication, *Area Economic Projections, 1990,* 177 economic regions are delineated. These are neither subdivided into smaller regions nor consolidated into larger regions.

     The more traditional procedure is to use state lines in order to outline the large economic regions of the United States. This practice simplifies the computation of data and allows the use of data that are available for states but not for counties. But it has the disadvantage that state lines are often unrealistic in the economic or political senses. They are legal boundaries which, under the Constitution of the United States, cannot be changed without the consent of the states involved. There have been only two changes in state boundaries since the Constitution was adopted, the separation of Maine from Massachusetts in 1820 and the separation of West Virginia from Virginia in 1861. The present practice is illustrated in the following list comparing the regions used by the Bureau of the Census and the Bureau of Economic Analysis. The second list shows how states have been classified in the present study.

## Bureau of The Census

1. New England . . . . . . . . . . . . . . . . . . . . . . . . . . Maine
                                                  New Hampshire
                                                  Vermont
                                                  Massachusetts
                                                  Rhode Island
                                                  Connecticut

2. Middle Atlantic . . . . . . . . . . . . . . . . . . . . . . . New York
                                                    New Jersey
                                                    Pennsylvania

3. East North Central . . . . . . . . . . . . . . . . . . . . Ohio
 Indiana
 Illinois
 Michigan
 Wisconsin

4. West North Central . . . . . . . . . . . . . . . . . . . Minnesota
 Iowa
 Missouri
 North Dakota
 South Dakota
 Nebraska
 Kansas

5. South Atlantic . . . . . . . . . . . . . . . . . . . . . . . Delaware
 Maryland
 District of Columbia
 Virginia
 West Virginia
 North Carolina
 South Carolina
 Georgia
 Florida

6. East South Central . . . . . . . . . . . . . . . . . . . . Kentucky
 Tennessee
 Alabama
 Mississippi

7. West South Central . . . . . . . . . . . . . . . . . . . Arkansas
 Louisiana
 Oklahoma
 Texas

8. Mountain ............................Montana
                                        Idaho
                                        Wyoming
                                        Colorado
                                        New Mexico
                                        Arizona
                                        Utah
                                        Nevada

9. Pacific .............................Washington
                                        **Oregon**
                                        California
                                        Alaska
                                        Hawaii

# Bureau of Economic Analysis

1. New England ........................Maine
                                        New Hampshire
                                        Vermont
                                        Massachusetts
                                        Rhode Island
                                        Connecticut

2. Mideast ............................New York
                                        New Jersey
                                        Pennsylvania
                                        Delaware
                                        Maryland
                                        District of Columbia

3. Great Lakes ........................Michigan
                                        Ohio
                                        Indiana
                                        Illinois
                                        Wisconsin

4. Plains . . . . . . . . . . . . . . . . . . . . . . . . . . . . . Minnesota
Iowa
Missouri
North Dakota
South Dakota
Nebraska
Kansas

5. Southeast . . . . . . . . . . . . . . . . . . . . . . . . . Virginia
West Virginia
Kentucky
Tennessee
North Carolina
South Carolina
Georgia
Florida
Alabama
Mississippi
Louisiana
Arkansas

6. Southwest . . . . . . . . . . . . . . . . . . . . . . . . Oklahoma
Texas
New Mexico
Arizona

7. Rocky Mountain . . . . . . . . . . . . . . . . . . . . . Montana
Idaho
Wyoming
Colorado
Utah

8. Far West . . . . . . . . . . . . . . . . . . . . . . . . . . Washington
Oregon
Nevada
California

9. Alaska and Hawaii . . . . . . . . . . . . . . . . . . . Alaska
Hawaii

## Economic Regions in this Study

1. Northeast Corridor ..................... Maine
   New Hampshire
   Massachusetts*
   Rhode Island
   Connecticut
   New York*
   New Jersey
   Pennsylvania*
   Delaware
   Maryland
   District of Columbia

2. Buffalo - Springfield ................... Vermont*

3. Pittsburgh - Detroit .................... Ohio*
   Michigan*

4. Chicago - Milwaukee ................... Illinois*
   Wisconsin*

5. Northwest ............................ Minnesota
   Iowa
   North Dakota
   South Dakota
   Montana*

6. Border Region ....................... Indiana*
   Kentucky
   West Virginia
   Missouri*
   Kansas**

7. Southeast ........................... Virginia*
   North Carolina
   Tennessee**
   South Carolina
   Georgia
   Florida
   Alabama*

8. Gulf . . . . . . . . . . . . . . . . . . . . . . . . . . . . Mississippi
                                            Louisiana
                                            Arkansas

9. Southwest . . . . . . . . . . . . . . . . . . . . . . . . . . Oklahoma*
                                            Texas*
                                            New Mexico
                                            Arizona*

10. Central West . . . . . . . . . . . . . . . . . . . . . . . Nebraska*
                                            Wyoming*
                                            Colorado*
                                            Utah

11. Northern Pacific . . . . . . . . . . . . . . . . . . . . Idaho*
                                            Washington
                                            Oregon
                                            Alaska

12. Southern Pacific . . . . . . . . . . . . . . . . . . . . . Nevada*
                                            California*
                                            Hawaii

*A majority of the state is in the region.
**A plurality of the state is in the region.

# Appendix B:
# Statistical Methods

This appendix contains the details that were used to estimate the proportions of the population of major metropolitan areas that are contained respectively by "old urbanized areas" (i.e., those developed prior to 1950) and "new urbanized areas" (i.e., those developed between 1950 and 1970).

In the case of minor metropolitan areas, it is probable that there are only two environments, the urbanized area proper and the outskirts. If one orders major metropolitan areas according to size, it becomes evident that the outskirts come to account for a larger part of the population of a metropolitan area as its size decreases. Thus, it is fairly easy to describe the structure of minor metropolitan areas with present statistical systems. One merely subtracts the population contained by the urbanized area from the entire population contained by the SMSA. The difference represents the outskirts, an area with accessibility to the urbanized portion of the SMSA where the population, however, resides at densities of less than 1,000 inhabitants per square miles or in satellite cities and towns with populations under 50,000. But as a metropolitan area increases in size, space begins to become scarcer. As a result, there develops a third, "large city" environment (which has been called the "core"), where population densities are substantially higher than for the rest of the urbanized area and which, as in the case of New York, the largest metropolitan area, contains as many as 12,500,000 inhabitants. Estimating the size and population density of the third environment presents many difficulties at present because there is no official definition of either its minimum size or its population density.

In this study the difficulties have not been overcome. No estimates of the "core" of major metropolitan areas are presented. Nevertheless, it has been possible to derive estimates of what has happened to the areas urbanized prior to 1950, and from this knowledge to describe the new urbanized areas. This information has been presented in the tables in Chapters 4 and 5. Before proceeding to describe the estimating methods one must emphasize, however, that in area statistics one must accept a much lower degree of precision than in national statistics. The problem, of course, is explained partly in statistical textbooks: namely, that as the size of what is being sampled decreases, sampling methods become more unreliable. What the textbooks leave out, however, is that "definitional" errors are also likely to increase so that survey and census techniques also become more unreliable. A "definitional" error arises from the fact that "enumerators" must have a definition of what they are supposed to count. Even with the clearest definitions, there will be some overcounting and some undercounting. Thus, according to the history of the 1960 Census of Population, there was an 8 percent undercount and a 5 percent overcount of the population, leaving a net 3 percent undercount. When one is counting a population of 200,000,000, however, the mistakes of enumerators are likely to cancel out. Some will use the definition more strictly and others more laxly. In area statistics, however, where there may be only two or three enumerators, there is no such margin for offsetting error in applying definitions, just as there is less room to reduce sampling error.

After estimating the outskirts of major metropolitan areas by subtracting the urbanized area from the 1970 SMSA, the next step taken was to use 1950 urbanized areas as the base from which to estimate the population of these same areas 20 years later. Appendix Table 1 makes it apparent that land area is not a problem. One has merely to subtract the 1950 land area of an urbanized area from its 1970 land area to derive how much new land was urbanized in these twenty years. The problem is population because some old urbanized areas increased their population density; some decreased it; and others experienced little change. Without knowledge of what happened to population densities, one cannot estimate the population of old urbanized areas in 1970.

Fortunately, there is a way of monitoring what has occurred in old urbanized areas because the Bureau of the Census publishes population density estimates for the urbanized portions of the central cities of metropolitan areas. Although central cities are political units and old urbanized areas are economic configurations, it is unlikely that trends in central cities and in old urbanized areas should differ widely. By taking the change in population density of central cities and applying it to the urbanized area of 1950, one should derive a rough-and-ready but serviceable estimate of the population residing within these urbanized areas in 1970. The main hitch to this procedure is that 29 of 58 central cities in these major metropolitan areas have annexed territory during the twenty years between 1950 and 1970. The population density of the annexed territory has been lower than that of the original territory, and thus the decline in population density is due in part to annexations, not merely to a lowering of population densities in the core. Thus, the foregoing procedure can be utilized without additional adjustments in one-half the cases studied in this report. For the other 29, one cannot simply extrapolate the change in population densities of central cities to the urbanized areas of 1950.

In 20 of these 29 cases where there have been annexations, the annexations have occurred in only one of the two census periods included between 1950 and 1970. This means that, in these 20 cases, there is some indication of the trends during these twenty years. In some cases, the data shows the trend from 1950 to 1960 and, in other cases, from 1960 to 1970. But trends in most major metropolitan areas have been stable from 1950 to 1970 (see Chapter 3). Urbanized areas that grew rapidly in one decade grew rapidly in the other. Thus, with minor hesitations, the trend during one census period has been used as representative of the entire trend over the two census periods from 1950 to 1970. On this basis, therefore, estimates of the old urbanized areas of 20 additional major metropolitan areas have been arrived at. They are less precise than in the 29 cases where there have been no significant boundary changes, but they serve as a rough approximation of the population in old urbanized areas that is better than any other available estimate.

The chief problem arises in the 9 cases where annexations have occurred in both the 1950-1960 census period and the 1960-1970 census period. Here there are no indications at all of the trends in the population densities of old urbanized areas. Thus, in these 9 cases (see Appendix Table 4), central city data are of little use. In both census periods, central cities lowered their population densities by annexing large portions of outlying territory settled at lower densities of population. In these cases, rather than merely subtracting the population of 1950 urbanized areas, an adjustment was possible that gave more precision to the estimate (even though it is based largely on past rates of growth). It is possible to derive the increase in rooms per person in the period from 1950 to 1970 from the Census of Housing. Without this adjustment, the population for 1950 of the urbanized areas of that date would probably be too high because, with rising income, people are occupying more rooms. Thus, the same building stock as existed in 1950 could not hold the same amount of people. Therefore, in the 9 cases where central city data provide no guidance, the population of old urbanized areas has been adjusted downward by the amount that rooms per person increased in the central city. They are very rough estimates because they do not take into account the change in the stock of housing, as do those where central city data have been used. Nevertheless, a comparison of the experience of most central cities for which there are data showing population trends indicates that this method of estimation, as rough as it is, will present an acceptable estimate of the population residing in old urbanized areas, an estimate that is slightly biased downward but not too far off the mark. If the population had not decreased in these old urbanized areas, then the data for central cities would show this fact, despite large annexations. Thus, it is possible to check for cases where, as in Los Angeles, the underestimate of the population would amount to 23 percent. This reduces the range of error to about 10 percent. Therefore, it is very unlikely that the population of the old urbanized areas in the 9 major metropolitan areas where there have been frequent annexations is underestimated by more than 10 percent.

**Appendix Table 1: Structure of Major Metropolitan Areas, Land Area 1970**

| | Total Urbanized Area | Old Urbanized Area | New Urbanized Area | Old Urbanized Area | New Urbanized Area |
|---|---|---|---|---|---|
| | (square miles) | | | (percent of total) | |
| Albany-Schenectady ....... | 151 | 54 | 97 | 35.8% | 64.2% |
| Allentown-Bethlehem ...... | 98 | 49 | 49 | 50.0 | 50.0 |
| Atlanta ................. | 435 | 106 | 329 | 24.4 | 75.6 |
| Baltimore .............. | 310 | 152 | 158 | 49.0 | 51.0 |
| Birmingham ............. | 225 | 100 | 125 | 44.4 | 55.6 |
| Boston ................. | 863 | 345 | 518 | 40.0 | 60.0 |
| Buffalo ................ | 214 | 101 | 113 | 47.2 | 52.8 |
| Chicago SCA ........... | 1,431 | 638 | 793 | 44.6 | 55.4 |
| Cincinnati ............. | 335 | 146 | 189 | 43.6 | 56.4 |
| Cleveland-Akron SCA ...... | 956 | 398 | 558 | 41.6 | 58.4 |
| Columbus, Ohio ......... | 234 | 65 | 169 | 27.8 | 72.2 |
| Dallas-Ft. Worth SCA ...... | 1,071 | 262 | 809 | 24.5 | 75.5 |
| Denver ................. | 307 | 105 | 202 | 34.2 | 65.8 |
| Dayton ................. | 224 | 63 | 161 | 28.1 | 71.9 |
| Detroit ................ | 872 | 395 | 477 | 45.3 | 54.7 |
| Grand Rapids ........... | 146 | 47 | 99 | 32.2 | 67.8 |
| Greensboro - Winston-Salem.. | 179 | 47 | 132 | 26.3 | 73.7 |
| Hartford ............... | 207 | 99 | 108 | 47.8 | 52.2 |
| Honolulu ............... | 115 | 85* | 30* | 73.9 | 26.1 |
| Houston ................ | 539 | 270 | 269 | 50.1 | 49.9 |
| Indianapolis ........... | 381 | 91 | 290 | 23.9 | 76.1 |
| Jacksonville ........... | 344 | 51 | 293 | 14.8 | 85.2 |
| Kansas City, Missouri....... | 493 | 149 | 344 | 30.2 | 69.8 |
| Los Angeles SCA ......... | 1,572 | 871 | 701 | 55.4 | 44.6 |
| Louisville .............. | 210 | 67 | 143 | 31.9 | 68.1 |
| Memphis ............... | 196 | 110 | 86 | 56.1 | 43.9 |
| Miami SCA ............. | 607 | 116 | 491 | 19.1 | 80.9 |
| Milwaukee ............. | 456 | 102 | 354 | 22.4 | 77.6 |
| Minneapolis-St. Paul ...... | 721 | 231 | 490 | 32.0 | 68.0 |
| Nashville .............. | 344 | 54 | 290 | 15.7 | 84.3 |
| New Haven ............. | 238 | 47 | 191 | 19.7 | 80.3 |
| New Orleans ............ | 184 | 103* | 81* | 56.0 | 44.0 |
| New York SCA ........... | 2,685 | 1,378 | 1,307 | 51.3 | 48.7 |
| Norfolk-Newport News SCA.. | 442 | 62 | 380 | 14.0 | 86.0 |
| Oklahoma City .......... | 339 | 67 | 272 | 19.8 | 80.2 |

# Appendix Table 1: (continued)

| | Total Urbanized Area | Old Urbanized Area | New Urbanized Area | Old Urbanized Area | New Urbanized Area |
|---|---|---|---|---|---|
| | (square miles) | | | (percent of total) | |
| Omaha | 151 | 66 | 85 | 43.7 | 56.3 |
| Philadelphia-Wilmington SCA | 862 | 358 | 504 | 41.5 | 58.5 |
| Phoenix | 388 | 55 | 333 | 14.2 | 85.8 |
| Pittsburgh | 596 | 254 | 342 | 42.6 | 57.4 |
| Portland, Oregon | 267 | 114 | 153 | 42.7 | 57.3 |
| Providence | 244 | 143 | 101 | 58.6 | 41.4 |
| Richmond | 145 | 48 | 97 | 33.1 | 66.9 |
| Riverside-San Bernardino | 310 | 61 | 249 | 19.7 | 80.3 |
| Rochester, N.Y. | 146 | 65 | 81 | 44.5 | 55.5 |
| Sacramento | 244 | 42 | 202 | 17.2 | 82.8 |
| Salt Lake City | 184 | 76 | 108 | 41.3 | 58.7 |
| San Antonio | 223 | 90 | 133 | 40.4 | 59.6 |
| San Diego | 381 | 133 | 248 | 34.9 | 65.1 |
| San Francisco-San Jose SCA. | 958 | 348 | 610 | 36.3 | 63.7 |
| Seattle-Tacoma SCA | 542 | 185 | 357 | 34.1 | 65.9 |
| Springfield, Mass. | 238 | 167 | 71 | 70.2 | 29.8 |
| St. Louis | 461 | 228 | 233 | 49.5 | 50.5 |
| Syracuse | 96 | 44 | 52 | 45.8 | 54.2 |
| Tampa-St. Petersburg | 291 | 111 | 180 | 38.1 | 61.9 |
| Toledo | 166 | 70 | 96 | 42.2 | 57.8 |
| Washington, D.C. | 494 | 178 | 316 | 36.0 | 64.0 |
| Worcester, Mass. | 84 | 44 | 40 | 52.4 | 47.6 |
| Youngstown-Warren | 129 | 79 | 50 | 61.2 | 38.8 |
| Total | 25,724 | 9,985 | 15,739 | 38.5 | 61.5 |

\* Estimated

Sources: 1970 and 1950 Censuses of Population.

# Appendix Table 2: Urbanized Portion of Central Cities without Significant Boundary Changes, 1950-1970

| | Urbanized Land Area 1950 | 1970 | Population Density 1950 | 1970 | Change in Population Density, 1950-1970 (percent) |
|---|---|---|---|---|---|
| | (square miles) | | (inhabitants per square mile) | | |
| Albany-Schenectady | 38.5 | 41.3 | 7,769 | 6,212 | −20.0% |
| Allentown-Bethlehem | 34.5 | 37.6 | 5,017 | 4,846 | − 3.4 |
| Baltimore | 78.7 | 78.3 | 12,067 | 11,568 | − 4.1 |
| Boston | 47.8 | 46.0 | 16,767 | 13,936 | −16.9 |
| Buffalo | 39.4 | 41.3 | 14,724 | 11,205 | −23.9 |
| Chicago | 207.5 | 222.6 | 17,450 | 15,126 | −13.3 |
| Cincinnati | 75.1 | 78.1 | 6,711 | 5,794 | −13.7 |
| Cleveland | 75.0 | 75.9 | 12,197 | 9,893 | −18.9 |
| Detroit | 139.6 | 138.0 | 13,249 | 10,953 | −17.5 |
| Hartford | 17.4 | 17.4 | 10,195 | 9,081 | −10.9 |
| Los Angeles | 450.9 | 463.7 | 4,370 | 6,073 | +40.0 |
| Miami | 34.2 | 34.3 | 7,289 | 9,763 | +33.9 |
| Minneapolis-St. Paul | 106.0 | 105.6 | 7,859 | 7,049 | −10.3 |
| New Haven | 17.9 | 18.4 | 9,187 | 7,484 | −18.5 |

| | Total Urbanized Area | Old Urbanized Area | New Urbanized Area | Old Urbanized Area | New Urbanized Area |
|---|---|---|---|---|---|
| | (square miles) | | | (percent of total) | |
| New Orleans ........ | 80.5 | 86.4 | 7,095 | 6,846 | — 3.5 |
| New York-Newark-<br>Jersey City ....... | 351.7 | 338.3 | 24,537 | 24,273 | — 1.1 |
| Philadelphia ........ | 127.2 | 128.5 | 16,286 | 15,164 | — 6.9 |
| Pittsburgh .......... | 54.2 | 55.2 | 12,487 | 9,422 | —24.5 |
| Providence .......... | 17.9 | 18.9 | 13,892 | 9,482 | —31.8 |
| Rochester, N.Y. ..... | 36.0 | 36.7 | 9,236 | 8,072 | —12.6 |
| Salt Lake City ...... | 53.9 | 59.3 | 3,379 | 2,966 | —12.2 |
| San Francisco-Oakland | 97.6 | 98.8 | 11,885 | 10,903 | — 8.3 |
| Seattle ............. | 70.8 | 83.6 | 6,604 | 6,350 | — 3.8 |
| Springfield ......... | 52.7 | 52.6 | 4,119 | 4,069 | — 1.2 |
| St. Louis .......... | 61.0 | 61.2 | 14,046 | 10,167 | —27.7 |
| Syracuse ........... | 25.3 | 25.8 | 8,719 | 7,644 | —12.3 |
| Washington, D.C. ... | 61.4 | 61.4 | 13,065 | 12,321 | — 5.7 |
| Worcester, Mass. ..... | 37.0 | 37.4 | 5,500 | 4,721 | —14.2 |
| Youngstown-Warren .. | 32.8 | 33.6 | 5,132 | 4,160 | —18.9 |

Sources: 1950, 1960, and 1970 Censuses of Population.

**Appendix Table 3: Urbanized Portion of Central Cities with Significant Boundary Changes in Only One Census Period, 1950-1970**

| | Urbanized Land Area | | | Population Density | | |
|---|---|---|---|---|---|---|
| | 1950 | 1960 | 1970 | 1950 | 1960 | 1970 |
| | (square miles) | | | (inhabitants per square mile) | | |
| Atlanta ............. | 36.9 | 128.0 | 131.5 | 8,979 | 3,308 | 3,779 |
| Birmingham ....... | 65.3 | 62.9 | 79.5 | 4,993 | 5,420 | 3,785 |
| Dallas ............. | 112.0 | 254.0 | 265.6 | 3,879 | 2,676 | 3,179 |
| Denver ............ | 66.8 | 71.8 | 95.2 | 6,224 | 6,879 | 5,406 |
| Dayton ............ | 25.0 | 34.1 | 38.3 | 9,755 | 7,693 | 6,360 |
| Greensboro ........ | 18.2 | 49.6 | 54.4 | 4,087 | 2,411 | 2,648 |
| Honolulu .......... | .. | 83.9 | 83.9 | .. | 3,566 | 3,872 |
| Houston ........... | 160.0 | 321.0 | 397.0 | 3,726 | 2,923 | 3,102 |
| Jacksonville ....... | 30.2 | 29.9 | 344.3 | 6,772 | 6,723 | 1,505 |
| Louisville ......... | 39.9 | 59.2 | 60.0 | 9,251 | 6,599 | 6,025 |
| Memphis .......... | 104.2 | 129.2 | 177.5 | 3,800 | 3,851 | 3,513 |
| Milwaukee ......... | 50.0 | 89.8 | 95.0 | 12,748 | 8,255 | 7,548 |
| Norfolk ........... | 28.2 | 50.2 | 52.6 | 7,571 | 6,073 | 5,855 |
| Omaha ............ | 40.7 | 47.8 | 76.6 | 6,170 | 6,310 | 4,534 |
| Phoenix ........... | 17.1 | 187.4 | 247.9 | 6,247 | 2,343 | 2,346 |
| Portland, Oregon .... | 64.1 | 66.2 | 89.1 | 5,829 | 5,630 | 4,294 |
| Richmond ......... | 37.1 | 37.7 | 60.3 | 6,208 | 5,834 | 4,140 |
| San Bernardino ..... | 19.5 | 25.2 | 44.4 | 3,234 | 3,684 | 2,348 |
| San Diego ......... | 99.4 | 194.7 | 212.8 | 3,364 | 2,944 | 3,261 |
| Tampa-St. Petersburg . | 71.2 | 121.8 | 139.9 | 3,110 | 3,746 | 3,531 |

Sources: 1950, 1960, and 1970 Censuses of Population.

## Appendix Table 4: Estimated Change in Dwelling Space per Inhabitant of Old Urbanized Areas, 1950-1970

| | Rooms per Person (Central City) 1950 (est.) 1970 | | Change in Rooms per Person, 1950-1970 | Preliminary Estimate of Population in Old Urbanized Areas[1] (Thousands) |
|---|---|---|---|---|
| Albany-Schenectady | 1.66 | 1.96 | 18% | 243.7 |
| Allentown-Bethlehem | 1.68 | 1.96 | 17 | 189.9 |
| Atlanta | 1.31 | 1.55 | 18 | 423.2 |
| Baltimore | 1.55 | 1.77 | 10 | 1,046.7 |
| Birmingham | 1.34 | 1.75 | 31 | 332.3 |
| Boston | 1.48 | 1.61 | 9 | 2,030.4 |
| Buffalo | 1.62 | 1.93 | 19 | 659.5 |
| Chicago, SCA | 1.37 | 1.55 | 13 | 4,301.4 |
| Cincinnati, SCA | 1.24 | 1.71 | 38 | 572.7 |
| Cleveland-Akron, SCA | 1.42 | 1.63 | 15 | 1,522.1 |
| Columbus, Ohio[2] | 1.47 | 1.67 | 14 | 379.0 |
| Dallas-Ft. Worth, SCA | 1.36 | 1.60 | 18 | 712.0 |
| Denver | 1.44 | 1.70 | 18 | 415.6 |
| Dayton | 1.42 | 1.69 | 19 | 286.7 |
| Detroit | 1.48 | 1.70 | 15 | 2,278.8 |
| Grand Rapids[2] | 1.62 | 1.80 | 11 | 202.5 |
| Greensboro - Winston-Salem | 1.35 | 1.61 | 19 | 145.3 |
| Hartford | 1.43 | 1.58 | 10 | 381.9 |
| Honolulu | 1.03 | 1.25 | 21 | 215.0 |
| Houston | 1.35 | 1.55 | 15 | 604.4 |
| Indianapolis[2] | 1.39 | 1.58 | 14 | 478.1 |
| Jacksonville | 1.45 | 1.86 | 28 | 185.4 |
| Kansas City, Missouri[2] | 1.52 | 1.75 | 15 | 598.7 |
| Los Angeles, SCA | 1.43 | 1.62 | 13 | 3,492.9 |
| Louisville | 1.25 | 1.73 | 38 | 332.9 |
| Memphis | 1.35 | 1.53 | 13 | 354.8 |
| Miami | 1.39 | 1.30 | —7 | 498.5 |
| Milwaukee | 1.55 | 1.60 | 3 | 805.3 |
| Minneapolis-St. Paul | 1.54 | 1.74 | 13 | 860.9 |
| Nashville[2] | 1.38 | 1.67 | 21 | 210.0 |
| New Haven | 1.48 | 1.77 | 20 | 200.7 |
| New Orleans | 1.19 | 1.43 | 20 | 504.8 |
| New York, SCA | 1.25 | 1.44 | 15 | 10,893.3 |
| Norfolk-Newport News, SCA | 1.32 | 1.58 | 20 | 315.7 |
| Oklahoma City[2] | 1.46 | 1.75 | 20 | 225.4 |
| Omaha | 1.39 | 1.58 | 14 | 268.6 |
| Philadelphia, SCA | 1.65 | 1.87 | 13 | 2,717.7 |
| Phoenix | 1.29 | 1.51 | 17 | 181.7 |
| Pittsburgh | 1.38 | 1.68 | 22 | 1,232.1 |
| Portland, Oregon | 1.68 | 1.85 | 10 | 461.8 |
| Providence | 1.47 | 1.70 | 16 | 495.4 |
| Richmond | 1.47 | 1.69 | 15 | 221.2 |
| Riverside-San Bernardino | 1.47 | 1.63 | 11 | 121.0 |
| Rochester, N.Y. | 1.55 | 1.75 | 13 | 357.6 |
| Sacramento[2] | 1.56 | 1.68 | 8 | 194.5 |
| Salt Lake City | 1.35 | 1.63 | 21 | 184.4 |
| San Antonio[2] | 1.16 | 1.38 | 19 | 371.2 |
| San Diego | 1.37 | 1.64 | 20 | 354.3 |
| San Francisco-San Jose, SCA | 1.52 | 1.71 | 12 | 1,940.1 |
| Seattle-Tacoma | 1.55 | 1.80 | 16 | 670.2 |

95

| | Rooms per Person (Central City) 1950 (est.) 1970 | | Change in Rooms per Person, 1950-1970 | Preliminary Estimate of Population in Old Urbanized Areas[1] |
|---|---|---|---|---|
| | | | | (Thousands) |
| Springfield, Mass. ......... | 1.47 | 1.63 | 11 | 318.1 |
| St. Louis ................ | 1.22 | 1.43 | 17 | 1,177.8 |
| Syracuse ............... | 1.59 | 1.89 | 19 | 219.2 |
| Tampa-St. Petersburg ...... | 1.52 | 1.81 | 19 | 242.9 |
| Toledo[2] ................ | 1.62 | 1.76 | 9 | 331.3 |
| Washington, D.C. .......... | 1.25 | 1.44 | 15 | 1,103.6 |
| Worcester, Mass. ........ | 1.61 | 1.74 | 8 | 201.4 |
| Youngstown-Warren ........ | 1.45 | 1.71 | 18 | 248.4 |

[1] This estimate is based on the assumption that the amount of dwelling space in a core has remained constant.

[2] The preliminary estimate has been adopted as final in these nine cases.

Sources: U.S. Census of Housing, 1950, 1960, 1970.

# Selected Conference Board Publications In Economic Policy Research

## A. Regional and Metropolitan Economic Research

### Articles in The Conference Board RECORD

de Torres, Juan. "Federal Aid to State and Local Governments," November, 1964.

—————. "Strengthening the Property Tax," May, 1965.

—————. "Local Government Expenditures: Postwar Determinants and Trends," February, 1966.

Levy, Michael E. "Trends and Prospects of Local Government Finances," October, 1966.

—————. "Planning-Programming-Budgeting," May, 1967.

de Torres, Juan and Smith, Delos R. "The Social Security Program in Perspective," May, 1968.

Levy, Michael E. and de Torres, Juan. "Federal Revenue Sharing," October, 1969.

Levy, Michael E. "Sharing Federal Revenue with the States—A Comparison of the ACIR and Nixon Proposals," April, 1970.

de Torres, Juan. "To Promote the General Welfare," July, 1972.

—————. "Nomenclature of the City," October, 1972.

—————. "Strains and Constraints on the (E)quality of Education," September, 1973.

—————. "Major Metropolitan Areas: New Market Patterns," January, 1974.

—————. "The New Reality of Major Metro-Areas," June, 1975.

—————. "The Changing Economies of Major Metropolitan Areas," August, 1975.

—————. "New York Is Really Something Different!" January, 1976.

*Studies*

de Torres, Juan. "Financing Local Government," *Studies in Business Economics,* No. 96, 1967.
——————. "Economic Dimensions of Major Metropolitan Areas: Population, Housing, Employment and Income," *Technical Paper,* No. 18, 1968.
Levy, Michael E. and de Torres, Juan. "Federal Revenue Sharing with the States: Problems and Promises," *Studies in Business Economics,* No. 114, 1970.
de Torres, Juan. "Government Services in Major Metropolitan Areas: Functions, Costs, Efficiency," *Research Report* No. 539, 1972.
Levy, Michael E., Editor. "Major Economic Issues of the 1970's," *CB Report,* 1973.

# B. Federal Budget and Fiscal Policy

### Articles in The Conference Board RECORD

Levy, Michael E. "Federal Budget: Trends and Projections," March, 1964.
——————. "Direct Impact of the 1964-65 Tax Cut," June, 1965.
——————. "Full Employment Without Inflation: A Trade-Off Analysis," December, 1966.
——————. "Full Employment Without Inflation: An Analysis of U. S. " 'Phillips Curves' and 'Target' Unemployment Rates," November, 1967.
——————. "Fiscal Push, Inflation, and the Budget Deficit," June, 1968.
——————. "Tax Surcharges, Spending Cuts, and Real Growth," October, 1968.
Levy, Michael E. and Smith, Delos R. "Vietnam and the Cost of Defense," July, 1969.
——————. "Reforming the Federal Budget Process," February, 1970.
Levy, Michael E. "The Vietnam Peace Dividend: Its Size, Distribution and Impact," August, 1970.
——————. "The Federal Budget in Transition: Managing Government Priorities," September, 1970.
Massaro, Vincent G. "The Expanding Role of Federally Sponsored Agencies," April, 1971.
Levy, Michael E. "Government Finance: A New Phase," April, 1973.
——————. "The CEA's 1974 Economy," March, 1974.
——————. "The 1974 Economy and the New Federal Budget," April, 1974.
——————. "In Quest of Price Stability," October, 1974.
Levy, Michael E. and Smith, Delos R. "The Congressional Budget Process Again Reformed," March, 1975.
Levy, Michael E. "America's Economy at the Crossroads," April, 1975.
——————. "The 1977 Federal Budget: Strategy for Containment," April, 1976.

*Studies*

Levy, Michael E. "Fiscal Policy, Cycles and Growth," *Studies in Business Economics,* No. 81, 1963.
Levy, Michael E., de Torres, Juan, and Smith, Delos R. *Federal Budget: Its Impact on the Economy* (Fiscal 1968 Edition) 1967; (Fiscal 1969-1977 Editions) 1968-1976.

# C. Monetary Policy and Financial Markets

*Articles in The Conference Board RECORD*

Kardouche, George K. "Monetary Ease During the 1961-65 Expansion," August, 1965.

——————. "Domestic Economic Policy and the U.S. Balance of Payments," August, 1966.

Levy, Michael E. "Monetary Pilot Policy, Growth, and Inflation," January, 1969.

——————. " 'Tight Money' or 'Credit Crunch,' " July, 1969.

Massaro, Vincent G. "Eurodollars and U.S. Banks," October, 1970.

Levy, Michael E. "U.S. Inflation and Wage-Price Guideposts," June, 1971.

Massaro, Vincent G. "Eurodollars and the U.S. Money Supply," September, 1971.

——————. "The Future of the Securities Industry," February, 1972.

Levy, Michael E. "From Phase 1 to Phase 3," June, 1972.

Massaro, Vincent G. "A New Financial Structure for the U.S.?" June, 1972.

——————. "Currency Crises and U.S. Interest Rates," August, 1972.

——————. "On the Making of Money," September, 1973.

Massaro, Vincent G. and Owusu, Stephen A. "Interest Rates in 1974," February, 1974.

Massaro, Vincent G. "Is the U.S. Facing a Capital Shortage?" January, 1975.

——————. "Controlling Money in 1975," May, 1975.

Levy, Michael E. "Constraining Inflation: Concerns, Complacencies, and Evidence," October, 1975.

Massaro, Vincent G. "Is There Enough Money?" November, 1975.

Owusu, Stephen A. "Interest Rates in 1976," February 1976.

Massaro, Vincent G. "Toward a New Financial Structure for the United States," February, 1976.

*Studies*

Levy, Michael E. "Cycles in Government Securities I. Federal Debt and Its Ownership," *Studies in Business Economics,* No. 78, 1962.

——————. "Cycles in Government Securities II. Determinants of Changes, in Ownership," *Studies in Business Economics,* No. 88, 1965.

Kardouche, George K. "The Competition for Savings," *Studies in Business Economics,* No. 107, 1969.

——————. "New Basic Data for the Analysis of Savings, 1952-1966," *Technical Paper,* No. 20, 1970.

Levy, Michael E., Editor. "Containing Inflation in the Environment of the 1970's," *Research Report* No. 519, 1971.

Massaro, Vincent G. "A Guide to Forecasting Interest Rates," *Research Report* No. 601, 1973.

# Bibliography

Banfield, Edward C. and Martin Grodzins. *Government and Housing in Major Metropolitan Areas.* New York: McGraw-Hill Book Company, 1958.

Bean, Walton A. *California, The Interpretive History.* New York: McGraw-Hill Book Company, 1968.

Blumenfeld, Hans J. *The Modern Metropolis.* Cambridge, Massachusetts: The MIT Press, 1967.

Chinitz, Benjamin. *Freight and the Metropolis.* Cambridge, Massachusetts: Harvard University Press, 1960.

Creamer, Daniel. *Manufacturing Employment by Type of Location.* New York: The Conference Board, 1969.

de Torres, Juan. *Economic Dimensions of Major Metropolitan Areas.* New York: National Industrial Conference Board, 1968.

Ezell, John Samuel. *The South Since 1865.* London: The Macmillan Company, 1963.

Gottman, Jean. *Megalopolis.* Cambridge, Massachusetts: The MIT Press, 1964.

Lubove, Roy. *The Urban Community.* Englewood Cliffs, New Jersey: Prentice-Hall, Inc., 1967.

Kuznets, Simon and Ernest Rubin. *Immigration and the Foreign Born.* New York: National Bureau of Economic Research, 1954.

Locklin, D. Philip. *Economies of Transportation.* Homewood, Illinois: Richard D. Irwin, Inc., 1972.

Passer, Harold C. *The Electrical Manufactures, 1875-1900.* Cambridge, Massachusetts: Harvard University Press, 1953.

Pomeroy, Earl. *The Pacific Slope, A History.* Seattle: University of Washington Press, 1973.

Tarbell, Ida. *Nationalizing of Business, 1878-1898.* New York: The Macmillan Company, 1956.

Turner, Frederick J. *The Frontier in American History.* New York: Henry Holt and Company, 1950.

# Index

## A.
"Advanced Services," 18-19, 58
Annexation, 25

## B.
BALD, F. CLEVER, 75n
BEAN, WALTON H., 67n
BOGUE, DONALD J., 83
BERRY, BRIAN J. L., 7
Bureau of Labor Statistics, 31n

## C.
Census of Population, 4-5, 31, 83
Central Business District, 9
Central Cities, 90-92
CHINITZ, BENJAMIN, 32
City Beautiful, 28-29
Civil War, 23, 32, 45, 50, 69
COLEMAN, E. J., 10n
Consumer Markets, 8-9

## D.
Depression, 24, 28, 30

## E.
EASTAL, R. C., 28n
Economic Development, 4, 8, 31
Electric Traction, 26
External Economies, 59

## F.
FOGELSON, ROBERT M., 28n
France, 69

## G.
GOTTMAN, JEAN, 55
Great Britain, 69
Greenfield Developments, 59

## H.
HAVIGHURST, WALTER, 78n
Heartland, 32, 69-70
HOLMES, OLIVER WENDELL, 50

## I.
Immigration, 24-25
Industrial Markets, 8-9, 12
Interstate Highway System, 45

Interurban Transportation, 15, 25
Intraurban Transportation, 25-27

## L.
Labor Markets, 10, 18
LEIBOWITZ, IRVING, 78n
LINCOLN, ABRAHAM, 4
Los Angeles, 28, 30, 65-66

## M.
Major Metropolitan Areas, 7, 14
Manhattan, 55-56
Manufacturing, 17, 23, 31-32, 40
Manufacturing Belt, 23, 33, 46, 66
MARSHALL, ALFRED, 20
Mass Transportation, 26, 27
McREYNOLDS, EDWIN C., 75n
Metropolitan Migration, 46-48, 73-74
Midwest, 23, 24
Minor Metropolitan Areas, 7, 13-14

## N.
NESBITT, ROBERT C., 78n
New England, 27, 28n, 56-57
New West, 70-71
A. C. Nielsen Co., 9
Nonmetropolitan Sector, 7, 14-16
North, 23, 24, 29, 32, 33-34, 38, 40-42
Northeast, 23, 24

## O.
Old West, 70
Outskirts, 6, 15, 27, 33-34, 89

## P.
PACKARD, VANCE, 39n
Peninsular Florida, 61-62
POMEROY, EARL, 68n
Population Densities, 46
Practical Intelligence, 10-11
PRED, ALLAN R., 24n

## Q.
Quota Acts, 25

## R.
Railroads, 23
Rimland, 50, 54-55, 69
Rural and Small-town America, 15, 24

## S.

Services, 31
SMITH, ADAM, 24
South, 23, 27-28, 32, 37-38, 43-45, 50, 71
SPRAGUE, FRANK J., 26
Standard Industrial Code, 16
Standard Metropolitan Statistical
    Area, 5-6
Suburbs, 26, 30

## T.

Technique, 10-11
TOOLE, K. ROSS, 78n
TOSDALE, HARRY F., 8

TURNER, FREDERICK JACKSON, 32

## U.

Urban Places, 16
Urbanized Area, 5-6, 33-34

## W.

West, 23, 32, 35-36, 38, 42-43
World War I, 25
World War II, 28, 30, 38

## Z.

Zoning, 29